Lecture Notes in Computer Science 14484

Founding Editors

Gerhard Goos
Juris Hartmanis

Editorial Board Members

The series Lecture Notes in Computer Science (LNCS), including its subseries Lecture Notes in Artificial Intelligence (LNAI) and Lecture Notes in Bioinformatics (LNBI), has established itself as a medium for the publication of new developments in computer science and information technology research, teaching, and education.

LNCS enjoys close cooperation with the computer science R & D community, the series counts many renowned academics among its volume editors and paper authors, and collaborates with prestigious societies. Its mission is to serve this international community by providing an invaluable service, mainly focused on the publication of conference and workshop proceedings and postproceedings. LNCS commenced publication in 1973.

Regine Kadgien · Andreas Jedlitschka ·
Andrea Janes · Valentina Lenarduzzi ·
Xiaozhou Li

Editors

Product-Focused Software Process Improvement

24th International Conference, PROFES 2023
Dornbirn, Austria, December 10–13, 2023
Proceedings, Part II

Springer

Editors

Regine Kadgien
FHV Vorarlberg University of Applied Science
Dornbirn, Austria

Andreas Jedlitschka ⓘ
Fraunhofer Institute for Experimental Software Engineering
Kaiserslautern, Germany

Andrea Janes ⓘ
FHV Vorarlberg University of Applied Science
Dornbirn, Austria

Valentina Lenarduzzi ⓘ
University of Oulu
Oulu, Finland

Xiaozhou Li ⓘ
University of Oulu
Oulu, Finland

ISSN 0302-9743 ISSN 1611-3349 (electronic)
Lecture Notes in Computer Science
ISBN 978-3-031-49268-6 ISBN 978-3-031-49269-3 (eBook)
https://doi.org/10.1007/978-3-031-49269-3

This Springer imprint is published by the registered company Springer Nature Switzerland AG
The registered company address is: Gewerbestrasse 11, 6330 Cham, Switzerland

Paper in this product is recyclable.

Preface

On behalf of the PROFES Organizing Committee, we are proud to present the proceedings of the 24th International Conference on Product-Focused Software Process Improvement (PROFES 2023). The conference was held during December 11–13, 2022.

Following the previous editions, the main theme of PROFES 2023 was professional software process improvement (SPI) motivated by product, process, and service quality needs. The technical program of PROFES 2023 was selected by a committee of leading experts in software process improvement, software process modeling, and empirical software engineering.

This year, we received 82 submissions. After a thorough evaluation that involved at least three independent experts per paper, 21 full technical papers were selected together with 6 industrial papers, 8 short papers, and 1 poster paper. Each submission was reviewed by at least three members of the PROFES Program Committees.

Alongside the technical program, PROFES 2023 hosted a doctoral symposium, two workshops, and one tutorial. In total three papers were accepted for the doctoral symposium. The 2nd Workshop on Computational Intelligence and Software Engineering (CISE 2023) aimed to foster integration between the software engineering and AI communities, and to improve research results, teaching and mentoring, and industrial practice. 8 papers were selected for CISE 2023. The 2nd Workshop on Engineering Processes and Practices for Quantum Software (PPQS 2023) aimed to establish a community, fostering academic research and industrial solutions focused on quantum software engineering principles and practices for process-centric design, development, validation, and deployment and maintenance of quantum software systems and applications. 3 papers were selected for PPQS 2023.

We are thankful for the opportunity to have served as chairs for this conference. The Program Committee members and reviewers provided excellent support in the paper evaluation process. We are also grateful to all authors of submitted manuscripts, presenters, keynote speakers, and session chairs, for their time and effort in making PROFES 2023 a success. We would also like to thank the PROFES Steering Committee members for their guidance and support in the organization process.

December 2023

Regine Kadgien
Andreas Jedlitschka
Andrea Janes
Valentina Lenarduzzi
Xiaozhou Li

Organization

Organizing Committee

General Chairs

Regine Kadgien — FHV Vorarlberg University of Applied Sciences, Austria

Andreas Jedlitschka — Fraunhofer Institute for Experimental Software Engineering, Germany

Program Chairs

Andrea Janes — FHV Vorarlberg University of Applied Sciences, Austria

Valentina Lenarduzzi — University of Oulu, Finland

Short Paper and Poster Chairs

Javier Gonzalez Huerta — Blekinge Institute of Technology, Sweden

Matteo Camilli — Politecnico di Milano, Italy

Industrial Chairs

Jan Bosch — Chalmers University of Technology, Sweden

Ralph Hoch — FHV Vorarlberg University of Applied Sciences, Austria

Workshop and Tutorial Chairs

Helena Holmström Olsson — Malmö University, Sweden

Simone Romano — University of Salerno, Italy

Doctoral Symposium Chairs

Maria Teresa Baldassarre — University of Bari, Italy

Tommi Mikkonen — University of Helsinki, Finland

Journal First Chair

Sira Vegas   Universidad Politécnica de Madrid, Spain

Proceedings Chair

Xiaozhou Li   University of Oulu, Finland

Publicity Chairs

Dario Amoroso d'Aragona   Tampere University, Finland
Rahul Mohanani   University of Jyväskylä, Finland

Program Committee

Dario Amoroso d'Aragona   Tampere University, Finland
Fabio Calefato   University of Bari, Italy
Tomas Cerny   University of Arizona, USA
Marcus Ciolkowski   QAware GmbH, Germany
Maya Daneva   University of Twente, The Netherlands
Dario Di Nucci   University of Salerno, Italy
Michal Dolezel   Prague University of Economics and Business,
                                      Czechia
Matteo Esposito   University of Rome "Tor Vergata", Italy
Michael Felderer   German Aerospace Center (DLR), Germany
Xavier Franch   Universitat Politècnica de Catalunya, Spain
Carmine Gravino   University of Salerno, Italy
Helena Holmström Olsson   Malmö University, Sweden
Martin Höst   Malmö University, Sweden
Marcos Kalinowski   Pontifical Catholic University of Rio de Janeiro,
                                      Brazil
Terhi Kilamo   Tampere University, Finland
Michael Kläs   Fraunhofer IESE, Germany
Jil Klünder   Leibniz Universität Hannover, Germany
Marco Kuhrmann   Reutlingen University, Germany
Xiaozhou Li   University of Oulu, Finland
Tomi Männistö   University of Helsinki, Finland
Tommi Mikkonen   University of Jyväskylä, Finland
Sandro Morasca   Università degli Studi dell'Insubria, Italy
Sergio Moreschini   Tampere University, Finland
Maurizio Morisio   Politecnico di Torino, Italy

Juergen Muench	Reutlingen University, Germany
Rudolf Ramler	Software Competence Center Hagenberg, Austria
Simone Romano	University of Salerno, Italy
Nyyti Saarimaki	Tampere University, Finland
Darja Smite	Blekinge Institute of Technology, Sweden
Kari Systä	Tampere University of Technology, Finland
Davide Taibi	University of Oulu, Finland
Xiaofeng Wang	Free University of Bozen-Bolzano, Italy
Dietmar Winkler	ACDP & SBA Research & TU Wien, Austria

Program Committee Members (Poster and Short Papers)

Eduardo Guerra	Free University of Bolzen-Bolzano, Italy
Eriks Klotins	Blekinge Institute of Technology, Sweden
John Noll	University of Hertfordshire, UK
Giovanni Quattrocchi	Politecnico di Milano, Italy
Ehsan Zabardast	Blekinge Institute of Technology, Sweden
Panagiota Chatzipetrou	Örebro University, Sweden
Bogdan Marculescu	Kristiania University College, Norway
Davide Fucci	Blekinge Institute of Technology, Sweden
Sandro Morasca	Università degli Studi dell'Insubria, Italy
Francis Palma	University of New Brunswick, Canada
Fabian Fagerholm	Aalto University, Finland
Priscila Cedillo	Universidad de Cuenca, Ecuador
Kwabena Ebo Bennin	Wageningen University & Research, The Netherlands
Renata Carvalho	Eindhoven University of Technology, The Netherlands
Alessandro Marchetto	University of Trento, Italy

Program Committee Members (Industry Papers)

Anas Dakkak	Ericsson, Sweden
Hongyi Zhang	Chalmers University of Technology, Sweden
Torvald Mårtensson	Saab AB, Sweden
Aiswarya Raj	Chalmers University of Technology, Sweden
Benjamin Schwendinger	TU Wien, Austria
Daniel Rotter	University of Applied Sciences Vorarlberg, Austria
Daniel Ståhl	Ericsson, Sweden

Sandro Widmer   RhySearch, Switzerland
Rimma Dzhusupova   McDermott, USA
Simon Kranzer   Salzburg University of Applied Sciences, Austria
David Issa Mattos   Volvo Cars, Sweden

Contents – Part II

**2nd Workshop on Engineering Processes and Practices for Quantum
Software (PPQS'23)**

Doctoral Symposium

Contents – Part I

Machine Learning and Data Science

Software Analysis and Tools

Software Testing and Quality Assurance

Security, Vulnerabilities, and Human Factors

Poster

Metrics for Code Smells of ML Pipelines

Dolors Costal[(⊠)] [iD], Cristina Gómez[iD], and Silverio Martínez-Fernández[iD]

Universitat Politècnica de Catalunya, Jordi Girona 1-3, 08034 Barcelona, Catalonia, Spain
{dolors.costal,cristina.gomez,silverio.martinez}@upc.edu

Abstract. ML pipelines, as key components of ML systems, shall be developed following quality assurance techniques. Unfortunately, it is often the case in which they present maintainability issues, due to the experimentatal nature of data collection and ML model construction. To address this problem, this work in progress proposes initial metrics to measure the presence of code smells in ML pipelines. These metrics reflect good software engineering practices for code quality of ML pipelines.

Keywords: ML Pipeline · Code Smells · Metrics

1 Introduction

Machine Learning (ML) systems are software systems that "learn by analyzing their environment and taking actions, aiming at having an intelligent behaviour" [1]. Developing ML systems requires implementing the main component that performs multiple sequential phases to produce ML models (ranging from data collection to training and evaluating the models). This component is usually known as ML pipeline [2].

ML systems have a special capacity for incurring on maintenance problems since they present general software maintenance problems plus additional ML-specific issues [3]. There exist several works that identify frequent types of ML-specific maintenance issues [4] such as anti-patterns [3], debts or code smells [6] (for short, we will refer to those issues as code smells), requiring refactorings [5]. Also, there is tool support [7] for assessing the software quality in ML projects and measure specific code smells. Although metrics have been proposed for general software code smells (e.g. [8]), to the best of our knowledge, metrics proposals for dealing with specific ML pipelines code smells are currently scarce. The main goal of this work in progress is to provide a set of metrics for measuring the presence of ML pipelines' code smells. Currently, a first relevant subset of those smells is being addressed.

Research on measuring specific ML pipelines code smells is important, as it encompasses a major part of data scientists' workflow [2]. Being able to measure the degree of presence of those smells is a first step towards solving ML pipelines maintenance problems.

R. Kadgien et al. (Eds.): PROFES 2023, LNCS 14484, pp. 3–9, 2024.
https://doi.org/10.1007/978-3-031-49269-3_1

2 ML Pipelines

An ML pipeline is "the process that takes data and code as input, and produces a trained ML model as the output" [2]. An ML pipeline follows a set of sequential phases. More concretely, Fig. 1 presents the phases needed for data engineering, (i.e., data collection, data cleaning and data labeling) and for model development (i.e., feature engineering, model training and model evaluation). The figure is adapted from the life cycle of a ML model presented in [9].

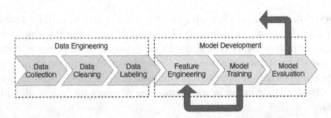

Fig. 1. Phases of ML pipelines (adapted from [9]).

When building an ML pipeline, decisions that data scientists make about the structure or architecture of the pipeline, the data types required to implement it, the ML libraries to use for favoring a rapid development of the pipeline and the configuration necessary for each phase, among other decisions, are key aspects to develop good quality ML pipelines with the absence of code smells.

3 Metrics for ML Pipelines Code Smells

This section presents some code smells that are specific of ML pipelines and proposes metrics to measure their presence. As a first step of this work in progress, we have addressed a subset of the code smells that are considered relevant in prior work [3–7] or have been shown prevalent in prior empirical studies [5, 6].

Glue Code. The building of ML models by ML pipelines is a complex activity that requires performing several tasks as, among others, data cleaning, ML algorithm selection and model optimization. The need of ML pipelines automation has led to the proliferation of ML libraries, such as, for example, TensorFlow[1], Keras[2], Scikit-learn[3] or PyTorch[4]. These libraries help data scientists to easily and quickly perform ML pipelines tasks to build their ML models. However, the use of those libraries requires a massive and specific supporting code to get data into and out of those libraries, resulting in a glue code smell [3]. The large amount of glue code in ML pipelines makes them "hard to comprehend, debug or even to enhance in the long run" [4].

---

[1] https://www.tensorflow.org
[2] https://keras.io/
[3] https://scikit-learn.org/stable/
[4] https://pytorch.org/

We propose the *Glue Code Ratio* metric (*GCR*) for glue code smells. *GCR* is the ratio between the number of lines of code for getting data out (*LOCOP$_i$*) and into (*LOCIP$_i$*) the parameters of each library call (represented by the index *i*), and the total lines of code (*LOC*) of the ML pipeline. The formula for the *GCR* metric is:

$$GCR = (\sum_{i=1}^{n} (\text{LOCIP}_i + \text{LOCOP}_i))/LOC$$

Values of the *GCR* close to 1 indicate a large presence of glue code while values close to 0 show the absence of the glue code smell.

Scattered Use of ML Library. This smell is related to the previous one because it also refers to the use of ML libraries. As mentioned in [6], this smell is about the disperse use of a ML library in multiple files. As a result, whenever this library needs to be updated or even replaced, developers have to make changes across several files.

We introduce the *Files Calling the Library l* metric (*FC$_l$*) for measuring the scattered use of the *l* ML library. The formula to calculate the values of this metric is:

$$FC_l = \text{number of files calling the library } l$$

Large values of *FC$_l$* metric point out the scattered use of the library *l* among the files composing the ML pipeline.

Dispensable Dependency. When developing a ML pipeline, sometimes developers test similar functions of a ML library or even from different ML libraries to choose the one that best fits the ML system requirements [6]. The dispensable dependency smell appears when some unused dependencies are left in the ML pipeline, adding unnecessary dependencies.

To measure this smell, we propose the *Unused Dependencies of a File f* metric (*UD$_f$*). Its formula is the following:

$$UD_f = \text{number of unusued libraries imported by the file } f$$

High values of *UD$_f$* metric indicate unneeded dependencies that should be removed.

Abstraction Debt. According to [3], "there is a distinct lack of strong abstractions to support ML systems" and "the lack of standard abstractions makes it all too easy to blur the lines between components". This is the case of ML pipelines where the absence of abstractions, encapsulation and modularization, make them difficult to understand and maintain. This means that components (i.e. files) often have not a clear functional delimitation and address several abstractions, something that in software engineering may indicate lack of cohesion and the presence of high coupling among different files.

An abstraction or concern is a relevant concept that has to be treated in a modular way to simplify the complexity of a software system. Much of the complexity and maintainability issues of ML pipelines come from the inadequate modularization of concerns or even from the lack of them [10].

We propose to take as indicative concerns the different phases of the ML pipeline presented in Sect. 2 (and obtained from the life cycle presented in [9]), namely, Data

Collection, Data Cleaning, Data Labeling, Feature Engineering, Model Training and Model Evaluation. These indicative concerns can be adapted or further refined for each specific pipeline according to its characteristics.

We define three metrics adapted from the ones presented in [10].

The *Diffusion of a Concern c* metric (DC_c) measures the spread of the concern c over the files of the ML pipeline. The formula to calculate this metric is:

$$DC_c = \text{number of files addressing the concern } c$$

A value of 1 in this metric represents an adequate modularization of the concern c since the concern is treated in a single file, whereas high values indicate the concern dissemination.

The *Coupling of a Concern c* metric (CC_c) assesses concerns dependencies (coupling between concerns) caused by concerns which are not well modularized. Its formula is the following:

$$CC_c = \text{number of other concerns with which the}$$
$$\text{concern } c \text{ shares at least a file}$$

High values of this metric for a concern c point out a high level of coupling for the concern.

The *Cohesion of a File f* metric (CF_f) measures the degree of cohesion of file f from the concerns point of view. Its formula is the following:

$$CF_f = \text{number of concerns addressed by the file } f$$

A value of 1 in this metric indicates a good level of cohesion of the file f, since the file is addressing a single abstraction. Higher values of this metric indicate mixing of concerns in the same file.

DC_c, CC_c and CF_f metrics are adapted from *Concern Diffusion over Architectural Components*, *Component-level Interlacing Between Concerns* and *Lack of Concern-based Cohesion* metrics, respectively, defined in [10].

Configuration Debt. "Any large [ML] system has a wide range of configurable options, including which features are used, how data is selected, a wide variety of algorithm-specific learning settings, etc." [3]. Sometimes, the lines of configuration exceed the lines of traditional code and principles of good configuration are not followed [3]. Configuration debt appears when "configuration (and extension of configuration) [is treated] as an afterthought" [3]. This suggests that configuration debt is a specific case of abstraction debt that applies to the configuration code and, therefore, the metrics proposed for abstraction debt may also measure the configuration debt. For example, when the *Diffusion of a Concern c* metric has a value greater than 1, the concern is spread in several files and it may indicate that the configuration corresponding to c may also be distributed among different files.

Plain-old Data Type Smell. The data used and produced by ML pipelines are usually represented as primitive types instead of separate data types or classes [3]. Excessive use of primitive types produces a disorganized code with hidden dependencies.

Plain-old data type smell is related to the primitive obsession smell defined for software systems in general. Two metrics defined for primitive obsession [11] may be directly applied to identify plain-old data type smell.

The *Method Parameters Clones of a File f* metric (MPF_f) [11] evaluates the excessive use of primitive types in method parameters of a file f. Its formula is:

$$MPF_f = \text{number of method parameters(with the same name and type)}$$
$$\text{that appear multiple times in the file} f$$

The *Static Final Primitives Usage of a File f* metric (SPU_f) [11] assesses the presence of variables in a file f that encode constant values for coding information. Its formula is:

$$SPU_f = \text{number of variables with}$$
$$\text{constant values as type codes in the file} f$$

High values of both metrics indicate the presence of many parameters and variables encoding constant values defined as primitive types.

4 Discussion

The metrics proposed can help data scientists to measure the presence of smells in ML pipelines, this being a first step to solve them. Some smells will be simple to solve, e.g., dispensable dependencies can be easily eliminated. Other smells, such as, abstraction debt or configuration debt involve the general organization of the code and can be more complex. Fortunately, there exist solutions from the software engineering discipline that may be used to reduce ML pipelines code smells.

The application of object-oriented design principles keeps software systems with low coupling and with high cohesion. For example, applying the Single Responsibility principle and the Dependency Inversion principle [12] to the files composing a ML pipeline favor a higher cohesion and lower coupling of the ML pipeline components and this will reduce both abstraction debt and configuration debt.

The application of object-oriented design patterns, such as, for instance, the adapter design pattern [13], to wrap in a single component the access to a ML library, reduces the presence of the scattered use of ML libraries code smell.

The plain old data type smell can be removed using code refactorings, as for example Replace Data Value with Object [14], by defining classes to encapsulate plain data types.

Regarding glue code, it must be recognized that the use of libraries can be necessary to avoid redundant work and, therefore, it is not always possible to reduce it. In those cases, it is advisable that the use of libraries is not scattered and that the needed glue code is designed in such a way that does not present other code smells.

5 Conclusions and Further Work

In this work in progress, we have identified ML-specific code smells that ML pipelines may exhibit and provided a set of metrics to measure the degree of their presence. These metrics represent a first step in the research needed to tackle the relevant issue of improving the quality of ML pipelines.

As future work, we aim to apply the metrics proposed to several scenarios to obtain relevant information that allows us to refine those metrics or even to include additional ones. We also plan to validate the proposed metrics with practitioners and to define code smells detection strategies, as detailed in [15], by combining the metrics introduced in this paper. Moreover, we want to add new ML-specific code smells and explore solutions, in the form of design patterns, to be applied for solving the ML-specific code smells. Finally, we want to implement a software service to compute the metrics to be integrated into tools that perform software quality evaluation.

Acknowledgements. This work was supported by the "Spanish Ministerio de Ciencia e Innovación" under project/funding scheme PID2020-117191RB-I00/AEI/10.13039/501100011033.

References

1. Martínez-Fernández, S., Bogner, J., Franch, X., Oriol, M., et al.: Software engineering for ai-based systems: a survey. TOSEM **31**(2), 1–59 (2022)
2. Continuous delivery for machine learning (2019). https://martinfowler.com/articles/cd4ml. html. Accessed 8 Mar 2023
3. Sculley, D., et al.: Hidden technical debt in machine learning systems. Adv. Neural Inf. Process. Syst. **28**, 2503–2511 (2015)
4. Jebnoun, H., Ben Braiek, H., Rahman, M.M., Khomh, F.: The scent of deep learning code: an empirical study. In: International Conference on Mining Software Repositories 2020, pp. 420–430 (2020)
5. Tang, Y., Khatchadourian, R., Bagherzadeh, M., Singh, R., Stewart, A., Raja, A.: An empirical study of refactorings and technical debt in machine learning systems. In: International Conference on Software Engineering (ICSE), pp. 238–250. IEEE (2021)
6. Gesi, J., et al.: Code smells in machine learning systems (2022). arXiv preprint arXiv:2203. 00803
7. Van Oort, B., Cruz, L., Loni, B., Van Deursen, A.: Project smells experiences in analysing the software quality of ML projects with mllint. In: International Conference on Software Engineering: Software Engineering in Practice, pp. 211–220 (2022)
8. Bafandeh Mayvan, B., Rasoolzadegan, A., Javan Jafari, A.: Bad smell detection using quality metrics and refactoring opportunities. J. Softw. Evol. Process **32**(8), 1–33 (2020)
9. Lewis, G.A., Ozkaya, I., Xu, X.: Software architecture challenges for ML systems. In: International Conference on Software Maintenance and Evolution (ICSME), pp. 634–638. IEEE (2021)
10. Sant'Anna, C., Figueiredo, E., Garcia, A., Lucena, C.J.: On the modularity of software architectures: a concern-driven measurement frame-work. In: Oquendo, F. (eds.) Software Architecture. ECSA 2007. LNCS, vol. 4758, pp. 207–224. Springer, Berlin, Heidelberg (2007). https://doi.org/10.1007/978-3-540-75132-8_17
11. Pengo, E., Gál, P.: Grasping primitive enthusiasm-approaching primitive obsession in steps. In: International Conference on Software Technologies, 2018, pp. 423–430 (2018)
12. Martin, R.C.: Design Principles and Design Patterns. https://web.archive.org/web/201509 06155800/http://www.objectmentor.com/resources/articles/Principles_and_Patterns.pdf. Accessed 23 July 2023
13. Gamma, E., Helm, R., Johnson, R., Vlissides, J.: Design Patterns. Elements of Reusable Object-Oriented Software, 1st edn. Addison-Wesley, Boston (1995)

14. Fowler, M.: Refactoring: Improving the Design of Existing Code, 2nd edn. Addison-Wesley, Boston (2019)
15. Lanza, M., Marinescu, R.: Object-Oriented Metrics in Practice: Using Software Metrics to Characterize Evaluate and Improve the Design of Object-Oriented Systems. Springer, Berlin, Heidelberg (2006). https://doi.org/10.1007/3-540-39538-5

Tutorials

Declarative Process Mining for Software Processes: The RuM Toolkit and the Declare4Py Python Library

Anti Alman[1]([⊠]) (iD), Ivan Donadello[2]([⊠]) (iD), Fabrizio Maria Maggi[2]([⊠]) (iD), and Marco Montali[2]([⊠]) (iD)

[1] University of Tartu, Tartu, Estonia
anti.alman@ut.ee
[2] Free University of Bozen-Bolzano, Bolzano, Italy
ivan.donadello@unibz.it, {maggi,montali}@inf.unibz.it

Abstract. Process mining is one of the research disciplines belonging to the field of Business Process Management (BPM). The central idea of process mining is to use real process execution logs in order to discover, model, and improve business processes. There are multiple approaches to modeling processes with the most prevalent one being the procedural models like Petri nets and BPMN models. However, procedural models can be difficult to use for processes like software processes that are highly variable and can have a high number of different branches and exceptions. In these cases, it may be better to use declarative models, because declarative models do not aim to model the end-to-end process step by step, but they constrain the behavior of the process using rules thus allowing for more flexibility in the process executions. The goal of this paper is to introduce the main principles of declarative process mining (i.e., process mining based on declarative models) and to show which state-of-the-art declarative process mining techniques have been implemented in the RuM toolkit and in the DECLARE4PY Python library.

Keywords: Declarative Process Mining · Software Processes · Process Discovery · Conformance Checking · Process Modeling

1 Introduction

Business Process Management (BPM) has become an integral part of how companies organize their workflows starting from the higher levels of management as recommended in ISO 9000, ISO 9001 Quality Management Principles (especially principles 4, 5, and 6)[1] to modeling and optimizing lower level processes through the use of various process mining techniques [1]. Process mining is the part of BPM which is focused on the analysis of business processes based on event

---

[1] International Organization for Standardization, *ISO quality management principles*, 2015: https://www.iso.org/files/live/sites/isoorg/files/store/en/PUB100080.pdf.

R. Kadgien et al. (Eds.): PROFES 2023, LNCS 14484, pp. 13–19, 2024.
https://doi.org/10.1007/978-3-031-49269-3_2

logs containing information about process executions. Process mining techniques are usually divided into three main branches which are process discovery, conformance checking, and process enhancement. Process discovery is used to generate a model of the process based on an event log of the process. Conformance checking is used to compare an event log to a process model with the aim of finding discrepancies between the event log and the model. Process enhancement is used to modify the model based on the information retrieved from the event log.

Process models can be divided into two types. The most common type includes procedural models like Petri nets and BPMN models, which aim to describe end-to-end processes and allow only for activities that are explicitly triggered in the control-flow [4]. However, modeling step by step the entire control-flow can be undesirable in some cases. For example, for software processes that are less structured and can have a high number of different branches and exceptions, the model could become quickly unreadable. For these processes, it may be a better choice to use declarative process models that model the process as a set of constraints that the process should follow. Declarative process mining techniques are process mining techniques based on declarative process models.

This paper presents two tools RuM [3] and DECLARE4PY [13] that make some of the existing declarative process mining techniques more accessible to a wider range of specialists, by focusing, in particular, on the declarative modeling language DECLARE [21]. RuM[2] is a Java application providing an easy-to-use GUI. DECLARE4PY[3] is a Python API that can be easily integrated in other Python applications. The two tools cover similar declarative process mining functionalities with minor differences.

2   Background

This section provides the necessary background on concepts that are crucial for understanding the research topic of this paper. It includes an overview of the process mining artifacts and covers the basics of DECLARE.

2.1   Event Logs, Traces, and Events

Process mining uses data collected from the information systems that leave their footprint during the executions of the processes they support in the so-called event logs. An *event log* is a set of traces. A *trace* is an execution of a business process. A trace contains a sequence of events, where each *event* is related to the execution of an *activity*, performed at a certain *timestamp* with a (possible) set of other attributes a.k.a. the *payload* of the event. Two traces belong to the same *variant*, if the sequence of activities corresponding to the events in the two traces are the same.

---

[2] https://rulemining.org.
[3] https://declare4py.readthedocs.io/en/.

2.2 Declare

DECLARE is a modeling language that uses a constraint-based declarative approach to define a loosely-structured process model [21]. The language is grounded in Linear Temporal Logic for finite traces (LTL_f) [10], but no knowledge of temporal logics is required to use the language effectively. The aim of the language is to describe a process in such a way that all the important aspects of the process are defined (such as activity A occurs immediately after activity B), while not requiring the entire process with all of its details to be modeled.

The main building blocks of the language are constraints. Each constraint consists of a template (a constraint type) and a reference to one or two activities depending on the template. A template basically defines the semantic meaning of the constraint and activities in the constraint define the activities to which this meaning applies. For example, if the constraint template is EXACTLY1 and the activity is A then this means that activity A should be performed exactly once during a single process execution.

When working with DECLARE constraints, it is important to understand three main concepts, which are constraint *activation*, constraint *fulfillment*, and constraint *violation*. For each constraint, there is at least one activity that is considered the activation of the constraint. If the activation occurs during the process execution then the corresponding constraint is considered to be activated. The occurrence of an activation triggers some obligations on the occurrence of another activity (the target). For example, for the RESPONSE constraint having A as activation and B as target, the execution of A forces B to be executed eventually after A. When a constraint is activated then it must be either fulfilled or violated by the end of the process execution. An activated constraint will be fulfilled when the condition defined by the constraint is satisfied, otherwise the constraint will be violated. If a constraint is not activated during the process execution then the constraint is considered to be vacuously satisfied [22].

MP-DECLARE [6] is an extension of DECLARE allowing the modeler to specify data conditions on the payload of the activation and/or of the target of a constraint.

3 RuM and Declare4Py

In this section, we list the declarative process mining techniques implemented in the RuM toolkit and the DECLARE4PY Python library. Both tools rely on well-known standards for the input and the output files, i.e., XES [14] for event logs and decl [23] for DECLARE models. This ensures their interoperability with other libraries and tools.

3.1 Features of the Tools

RuM currently has five major features: *process discovery, conformance checking, process monitoring, log generation,* and *log filtering*. RuM also provides a DECLARE editor. DECLARE4PY has five major features: *process discovery, conformance checking, query checking, log generation,* and *log filtering*.

Process Discovery. RuM implements four methods for process discovery: DECLARE MINER, MINERFUL, MP-DECLARE MINER, and MP-MINERFUL. DECLARE MINER [16] and MINERFUL [12] are well established discovery algorithms for DECLARE. The other two algorithms [15,17] are focused on MP-DECLARE and have an additional post-processing step to discover data conditions from the event log. The result of the discovery task are presented in three different formats: as a DECLARE model, as a textual description of the discovered constraints, and as an automaton representing the translation into an automaton of the LTL_f semantics of the discovered model. The discovery method supported by DECLARE4PY is the (data-agnostic) DECLARE MINER only. The results are returned in a Python data structure containing, for each constraint of the discovered model, the traces that satisfy it. A DECLARE4PY function allows the user to filter such data structure to retrieve the most frequently satisfied constraints.

Conformance Checking. In RuM, conformance checking is supported by three methods: DECLARE ANALYZER, DECLARE REPLAYER, and DATA-AWARE DECLARE REPLAYER. The DECLARE ANALYZER, introduced in [6], takes a model and an event log as inputs and returns activations, violations, and fulfillments in each trace in the log of each constraint in the model. The DECLARE REPLAYER [9] and the DATA-AWARE DECLARE REPLAYER [5] report trace alignments (using as inputs models without and with the data perspective, respectively). The results are grouped by trace or by constraint. If the results are grouped by trace, the details of a group show how the selected trace is affected by each constraint in the model. If the results are grouped by constraint, the details of a group show how that specific constraint affects each trace in the event log. The conformance checking method supported by DECLARE4PY is the DECLARE ANALYZER. The results are listed in a Python data structure indexed by trace identifier. The user can easily query such data structure to retrieve or aggregate information.

Query Checking. This task follows the method presented in [18] and takes as input an event log, a support threshold, and an MP-DECLARE query (i.e., an MP-DECLARE constraint in which the activation and/or the target activity are unspecified and replaced with placeholders) and returns the set of assignments of activities to the placeholders such that the input query instantiated using those assignments is satisfied in a percentage of traces in the log higher than or equal to the support threshold. This task is only implemented in DECLARE4PY and returns a data structure containing the assignments.

Process Monitoring. RuM also provides a functionality for process monitoring. It allows users to animate a DECLARE model by replaying a log over the model and showing if each trace in the log violates or satisfies the constraints defined in the model while the trace develops. This allows users to simulate the log behavior over a DECLARE model, observe and identify where the constraints are temporarily or permanently satisfied or violated after the occurrence of each event in the log. RuM supports three monitoring methods: MP-Declare w Alloy [19], MobuconLTL [20], and MobuconLDL [8].

Log Generation. Generating an artificial event log from a model can be useful for testing out new process mining algorithms or gaining a better understanding of how the process executions may look like based on the model. In RuM, the log generation supports the Alloy Log Generator [18], the ASP Log Generator [7], and the MINERful Log Generator [11], with the main difference being that the Alloy Log Generator and the ASP Log Generator methods can also account for the data perspective in the input model. Also Declare4Py provides a log generator based on ASP. The log generator available in Declare4Py has more advanced options with respect to the ones available in RuM. In particular, the tool is able to generate compliant and non-compliant (positive and negative) traces. The tool is also able to generate multiple variants of compliant and non-compliant traces. The user can specify how many variants should be generated and how many times the same variant should be repeated in the generated log. The tool also allows users to specify the number of times an activation of a constraint must occur in a trace.

Log Filtering. RuM and Declare4Py both provide features for log filtering. As basic filters the ones implemented in Disco[4] are available. A number of advanced filters based on LTL_f are also available. Some of them filter out traces that are not compliant with some predefined LTL_f rules that according to the literature [2] are relevant in the BPM context. Similarly, Declare constraints and Branched Declare[5] constraints can also be used for filtering.

4 Summary

In this paper, we presented the functionalities provided by the RuM toolkit and the Declare4Py Python library. These tools will be presented in a tutorial at PROFES 2023. The tutorial will provide a general overview of the main process mining tasks followed by a brief introduction to the existing declarative process mining techniques. In order to develop a mastery of these techniques, in the tutorial, we will introduce the tools presented in this paper and we will apply these tools to answer process-related questions using real-life datasets pertaining to software processes.

References

1. van der Aalst, W., et al.: Process mining manifesto. In: Daniel, F., Barkaoui, K., Dustdar, S, (eds.) BPM 2011. LNBIP, vol. 99, pp. 169–194. Springer, Heidelberg (2012). https://doi.org/10.1007/978-3-642-28108-2_19

---

4 https://fluxicon.com.

5 Branched Declare is an extension of Declare in which constraints are defined over disjunctions of activities.

2. van der Aalst, W.M.P., de Beer, H.T., van Dongen, B.F.: Process mining and verification of properties: an approach based on temporal logic. In: Meersman, R., Tari, Z. (eds.) OTM 2005. LNCS, vol. 3760, pp. 130–147. Springer, Heidelberg (2005). https://doi.org/10.1007/11575771_11
3. Alman, A., Di Ciccio, C., Haas, D., Maggi, F.M., Nolte, A.: Rule mining with RuM. In: ICPM, pp. 121–128 (2020)
4. Augusto, A., et al.: Automated discovery of process models from event logs: review and benchmark. IEEE Trans. Knowl. Data Eng. 31(4), 686–705 (2019)
5. Bergami, G., Maggi, F.M., Marrella, A., Montali, M.: Aligning data-aware declarative process models and event logs. In: BPM, vol. 12875, pp. 235–251 (2021)
6. Burattin, A., Maggi, F.M., Sperduti, A.: Conformance checking based on multi-perspective declarative process models. Expert Syst. Appl. 65, 194–211 (2016)
7. Chiariello, F., Maggi, F.M., Patrizi, F.: ASP-based declarative process mining. In: AAAI, pp. 5539–5547. AAAI Press (2022)
8. De Giacomo, G., De Masellis, R., Maggi, F.M., Montali, M.: Monitoring constraints and metaconstraints with temporal logics on finite traces. ACM Trans. Softw. Eng. Methodol. 31(4), 68:1–68:44 (2022)
9. De Giacomo, G., Maggi, F.M., Marrella, A., Patrizi, F.: On the disruptive effectiveness of automated planning for LTLf-based trace alignment. In: AAAI, pp. 3555–3561. AAAI Press (2017)
10. De Giacomo, G., Vardi, M.Y.: Linear temporal logic and linear dynamic logic on finite traces. In: IJCAI, pp. 854–860 (2013)
11. Di Ciccio, C., Bernardi, M.L., Cimitile, M., Maggi, F.M.: Generating event logs through the simulation of declare models. In: Barjis, J., Pergl, R., Babkin, E. (eds.) EOMAS 2015. LNBIP, vol. 231, pp. 20–36. Springer, Cham (2015). https://doi.org/10.1007/978-3-319-24626-0_2
12. Di Ciccio, C., Mecella, M.: On the discovery of declarative control flows for artful processes. ACM Trans. Manag. Inf. Syst. 5(4), 24:1–24:37 (2015)
13. Donadello, I., Riva, F., Maggi, F.M., Shikhizada, A.: Declare4Py: a python library for declarative process mining. In: BPM Demos. CEUR Workshop Proceedings, vol. 3216, pp. 117–121 (2022)
14. Gunther, C.W., Verbeek, H.: XES-standard definition (2014)
15. Leno, V., Dumas, M., Maggi, F.M.: Correlating activation and target conditions in data-aware declarative process discovery. In: Weske, M., Montali, M., Weber, I., vom Brocke, J. (eds.) BPM 2018. LNCS, vol. 11080, pp. 176–193. Springer, Cham (2018). https://doi.org/10.1007/978-3-319-98648-7_11
16. Maggi, F.M., Di Ciccio, C., Di Francescomarino, C., Kala, T.: Parallel algorithms for the automated discovery of declarative process models. Inf. Syst. 74(Part), 136–152 (2018)
17. Maggi, F.M., Dumas, M., García-Ba nuelos, L., Montali, M.: Discovering data-aware declarative process models from event logs. In: BPM, vol. 8094, pp. 81–96 (2013)
18. Maggi, F.M., Marrella, A., Patrizi, F., Skydanienko, V.: Data-aware declarative process mining with SAT. ACM Trans. Intell. Syst. Technol. (2023). https://doi.org/10.1145/3600106
19. Maggi, F.M., Montali, M., Bhat, U.: Compliance monitoring of multi-perspective declarative process models. In: EDOC, pp. 151–160 (2019)
20. Maggi, F.M., Montali, M., Westergaard, M., van der Aalst, W.M.P.: Monitoring business constraints with linear temporal logic: an approach based on colored automata. In: BPM, vol. 6896, pp. 132–147 (2011)

21. Pesic, M., Schonenberg, H., van der Aalst, W.M.P.: DECLARE: full support for loosely-structured processes. In: 11th IEEE International Enterprise Distributed Object Computing Conference (EDOC), pp. 287–300 (2007)
22. Schunselaar, D.M.M., Maggi, F.M., Sidorova, N.: Patterns for a log-based strengthening of declarative compliance models. In: IFM, vol. 7321, pp. 327–342 (2012)
23. Skydanienko, V., Di Francescomarino, C., Ghidini, C., Maggi, F.M.: A tool for generating event logs from multi-perspective declare models. In: BPM (Dissertation/Demos/Industry). CEUR Workshop Proceedings, vol. 2196, pp. 111–115. CEUR-WS.org (2018)

2nd Workshop on Computational Intelligence and Software Engineering (CISE 2023)

MaREA: Multi-class Random Forest for Automotive Intrusion Detection

Danilo Caivano[1], Christian Catalano[2], Mirko De Vincentiis[1(✉)], Alfred Lako[3], and Alessandro Pagano[1]

[1] University of Bari Aldo Moro, Bari, Italy
{danilo.caivano,mirko.devincentiis,alessandro.pagano}@uniba.it
[2] University of Salento, Lecce, Italy
christian.catalano@unisalento.it
[3] Polytechnic University of Tirana, Tirana, Albania
alfred.lako@fin.edu.al

Abstract. The technology inside modern vehicles is rapidly growing and poses newer security risks, as vehicle communication protocols are not yet fully secured and vulnerable to attacks. Consequently, the implementation of automotive cybersecurity systems has gained more attention. Controller Area Network (CAN) is one of the most studied communication protocols in the literature and lacks inherent cybersecurity measures. Several works proposed Intrusion Detection Systems (IDSs) using Machine Learning (ML) and Deep Learning (DL) algorithms to identify attacks on the CAN bus. Exploiting ML or DL techniques in a multi-class approach makes it possible to know the attack typology and to support developers' decisions to integrate concrete design methods in the software automotive development life-cycle. However, most automotive IDSs are tested on data sets that contain raw CAN messages without the possibility of decoding these messages to understand how the attack was generated. Based on these gaps, a Multi-class Random Forest for Automotive Intrusion Detection (MaREA) is presented, and a new Synthetic Automotive Hacking Dataset (SA-Hacking Dataset) is generated with a Database for CAN (DBC) file. First, the model is validated on the Car-Hacking dataset and compared with two other works in the literature that used the same classifier and dataset for the multi-class approach. Then, the Random Forest model is tested by concatenating the Survival Analysis Dataset and the SA-Hacking Dataset. The proposed approach presented better-quality results for both the Car-Hacking dataset and the aforementioned concatenated dataset.

Keywords: Automotive · Artificial Intelligence · Software Engineering · IDS

1 Introduction

The identification of cyber attacks in the automotive industry is growing faster as modern vehicles come integrated with potentially vulnerable entry points

R. Kadgien et al. (Eds.): PROFES 2023, LNCS 14484, pp. 23–34, 2024.
https://doi.org/10.1007/978-3-031-49269-3_3

such as Advanced Driver Assistance Systems (ADAS), Infotainment systems, OBD-II ports, and Bluetooth. It is necessary to preserve the confidentiality, integrity and availability of these systems to ensure the safety of people [8, 9,13] and this is also considering the increase in projects within smart cities involving smart mobility and autonomous driving [7]. They communicate with components of the Electronic Control Unit (ECU) using different protocols. The controller area network (CAN) is the most widely used communication protocol for transmitting information between ECUs and other buses connected through different gateways [11].

Although CAN is highly reliable and resistant to electromagnetic interference [39], it has been proven to have software vulnerabilities [21,26,28]. In particular, the protocol does not implement encryption and authentication techniques, making it vulnerable to several attacks [18]. Tencent Keen Security Research Lab showed critical vulnerabilities for Tesla, Mercedes and Lexus branded cars [1–4]. For example, in [1], they found that on the CAN bus, the head unit transmitted the Passphrase and Service Set Identifier (SSID) of Wi-Fi through the CAN bus as plain text to the T-Box component. In [3], researchers, while exploiting the ADAS system of a Tesla Model S, were able to craft an image to interfere and return improper results using an adversarial attack.

Several works in the literature exploit Intrusion Detection System-based techniques to prevent attacks on the bus. However, many of these approaches use binary classification without knowing the type of attack. Additionally, automotive classification models are fitted with data sets [39] that contain the same attacks (such as denial of service, fuzzing and spoofing). Furthermore, without the Database for CAN (DBC) file, the raw messages cannot be interpreted to understand the type of attack, except for reverse engineering techniques [17,27]. In addition, it is possible to reengineer the software ECUs in order to deploy an IDS model to identify attack CAN. For example, components embedded in NVIDIA [32] could be used as ECUs because they provide high computational resources and energy efficiency.

With these considerations, the paper presents the following contributions:

- The proposition of a multi-class approach using a Random Forest to detect attack injections on a CAN bus. The proposed model (MaREA, Multiclass Random Forest for Automotive Intrusion Detection) was tested in two steps: in the first step, comparing it with existing classifiers in the literature [22,25] using Random Forest and on the same dataset, Car Hacking Dataset, while in the second phase with the Survival Analysis Dataset and the Synthetic Automotive Dataset.
- The generation of a new synthetic automotive hacking data set with a custom DBC file that contains normal and fabrication attack messages. The fabrication attack was carried out based on the work of [19] in which an adversary forged a CAN message to override any periodic messages sent by a legitimate ECU.

The paper is organized as follows. Section 2 describes the related works; Sect. 3 presents the background of the CAN protocol and the Database for CAN necessary to understand the generated datasets and the dataset's attributes; Sect. 4 introduces the Car-Hacking Dataset, the Survival Analysis Dataset and how the SA-Hacking Dataset has been generated; Sect. 5 explains the experimental phase and the proposed approach describing the preprocessing phase and how the experiments are conducted, concluding with the evaluation of the results; finally, Sect. 6 presents the conclusion and future works.

2 Related Work

With the adoption of sophisticated components such as Advanced Driver Assistance Systems (ADASs) and Infotainment Systems, vehicles are becoming a target to demonstrate that these components are vulnerable. Miller and Valasek [29,30] showed that vehicles are vulnerable to cyberattacks. They could remotely control a Jeep Cherokee by exploiting vulnerabilities: getting the vehicle brake, moving the steering wheel, and turning on the radio. These works have led researchers to identify new attacks and defense techniques such as IDSs, Vehicle-SOC [12], or Quantum Artificial Intelligence to support developers' decisions to integrate concrete design methods in the automotive development life-cycle [20,36]. In particular, researchers have developed new IDSs based on the protocols used for in-vehicle networks [39]. Security solutions for IDSs in the vehicle field are focused on analyzing the messages exchanged between the ECUs that used the CAN protocol. The IDS approaches used Deep Learning (DL) or classical Machine Learning (ML) approaches. In [22], the authors compared different classical ML algorithms RF (random forest), K-NN (k-Nearest Neighbors) and XGBoost (Extreme Gradient Boosting) using the CAN-Intrusion-Dataset (also called Car-Hacking Dataset). Experiments have shown that the RF outperforms the KNN and XGBoost with an accuracy of 97%. Yang et al. [40] conducted similar work that considered the Decision Tree (DT), RF, Extra Trees (ET) and XGBoost and then an ensemble method using these models. The models were evaluated using two datasets: Car-Hacking Dataset and CIC-IDS2017. The second data set is unrelated to the automotive field because it is used for security testing and malware prevention (Web-Attack, Botnets, and Distributed Denial of Service (DDoS). The authors combined the model that obtained the best performance for the stacking method. RF, DT, and ET. The RF obtained the best metrics compared to DT and ET. Kalkan and Sahingoz [25] proposed an IDS using different ML algorithms (RF, Bagging Tree, Adaptive Boosting, Naive Bayes, Logistic Regression) and an Artificial Neural Network tested on the Car Hacking Dataset. The authors perform a binary and a multiclass classification. Alfardus and Rawat [6] used RF, KNN, and SVM as traditional ML algorithms and a multilayer perceptron (MLP) as a Deep Learning algorithm. Using the Car-Hacking Dataset, the authors obtained 100% precision with DoS, Gear, and RPM attacks. Instead, with the Fuzzy, the best results were obtained with RF and SVM. Furthermore, Han et al. [23] created a dataset called *Survival Analysis Dataset* that collects three CAN attacks: *Flooding*, *Fuzzy*, and *Malfunction*. The authors created an algorithm to determine whether the CAN message is not an attack by comparing the rate of the CAN ID with the ground truth. Using the same dataset, in [24], the authors proposed a deep learning model called Long Short-Term Memory (LSTM) in binary and multiclass approach. The researchers obtained better results in the binary approach than in the multiclass. In the survey by Rajapaksha et al. [34], the authors report a list of benefits and drawbacks considering the different ML algorithms used as IDS. The RF has better learning ability for small data, is able to train quickly, and has high model explainability. On the other hand, the drawback is that it has low accuracy compared to deep learning models, but it has been confirmed in the literature that RF obtained good accuracy [6,25]. Moreover, the drawback of the DL models is that they require high data to be fitted, and the datasets in the automotive field are extremely unbalanced (see Sect. 4). Taking into account other state-of-the-art machine learning models, such as SVM, it has better learning with small samples but is sensitive to kernel function parameters [34]. Moreover, in [31] the authors report a comparative analysis using different traditional machine learning algorithms such as RF and SVM. The results show that the RF obtained better results than the SVM.

Therefore, considering the related work and the considerations given above, RF was used as a traditional ML algorithm. Our model, MaREA, will be validated with [22,25] because the authors used a random forest in a multiclass approach with a state-of-the-art dataset. The Survival Analysis Dataset was used since both [23,24] dealt with this dataset. The results of the proposed methodology were compared only with [24] because it uses a multiclass approach instead of [23], which only uses binary classification.

3   Background

This section will briefly introduce the Controller Area Network (CAN) protocol and syntax in the Database for CAN (DBC). CAN [14] is the most used protocol for the in-vehicle network. The CAN is a broadcast protocol that allows ECUs to communicate and exchange messages between themselves. The protocol uses a bit-wise arbitration mechanism to avoid collisions when two or more messages are sent simultaneously. Considering two nodes, when these start the transmission of a frame, the messages with the lowest priority lose the arbitration, and the message with high priority can send the message on the bus. The priority of the message is determined by the Arbitration Field. The CAN protocol consists of different frames (Data, Remote, Error, and Overload), the most important being the *Data Frame*. The data frame is subdivided into different fields; the *identifier (ID)*, which is used for the arbitration phase; *Data Length Code (DLC)*, which is the length of the payload sent on the bus, and the *Data* which is the payload containing information about the message. Since the CAN protocol does not implement encryption or authentication mechanisms, it is vulnerable to different attacks such as denial of service, eavesdropping, and message injection [15,28]. In this paper, three different attack scenarios have been considered because they are the most analyzed in the literature: **Denial-of-Service**, an attacker sends high priority messages at a certain frequency rate to suspend communication between the ECUs [38]; **Fuzzy**, an attacker can craft malicious messages by injecting random ID or data into the CAN bus [38]; **Malfunction**, an attacker uses a specific ID to craft malicious messages by sending random data with a fixed value to cause a change in vehicle behavior [23].

4   Datasets

This section introduces the datasets used to evaluate the Random Forest. The Car Hacking Dataset, Survival Analysis Dataset, and the generated dataset called SA (Synthetic Automotive) Hacking Dataset are described, and the data attributes present in each are: *Timestamp*, is the recorded time; *CAN ID*, the message identifier in hexadecimal form; *DLC*, indicates the number of bytes from 0 to 8; *DATA*, the payload in hexadecimal form from DATA[0]-DATA[7]; *Flag*, **T** represents an injected message while **R** a normal message.

(i) Car-Hacking Dataset. Car hacking[1] [35,37] was published by the Hacking and Countermeasure Research Lab (HCRL) containing real CAN messages from a Hyundai YF Sonata car captured using an OBD-II port. The authors of the data set performed three attacks: Denial of Service (DoS), Fuzzy, and Spoofing. The spoofing attack uses the same methodology as the malfunction attack (see 3). The Car Hacking Dataset is subdivided into four datasets: DoS, Fuzzy, Spoofing RPM, and Spoofing Gear, each containing normal and attack messages. Table 1(a) shows the number of normal and attack messages for each dataset.

(ii) Survival Analysis Dataset. The Survival Analysis Dataset[2] [23] consists of Flooding, Fuzzy, and Malfunction attacks conducted on three vehicles: HYUNDAI YF Sonata, KIA Soul, and CHEVROLET Spark. In the flooding attack, an ECU overpopulates the CAN bus sending a large number of messages with the identifier set to *000*. In the fuzzy attack, the authors randomly generated IDs ranging from *0x000* to *0x7FF* every 0.0003 s. In the malfunction attack, a specific identifier was chosen for each vehicle type: *0x316* for the HYUNDAI YF Sonata, *0x153* for the KIA Soul and *0x18E* for the CHEVROLET Spark. Table 1(b) shows the number of normal and attack messages for the three datasets contained in the KIA Soul Dataset.

(iii) SA-Hacking Dataset. Cho and Shin [19] considered three attack scenarios on in-vehicle networks: Fabrication, Suspension, and Masquerade. Considering this, in this phase of the research work, only the fabrication attack is considered, where an adversary forged the identifier, DLC, and data of a specific CAN identifier message [10]. As reported by Cho and Shin, the objective of this attack is to override any periodic messages sent by a legitimate ECU. The SA-Hacking Dataset was generated on Ubuntu 20.04 with a virtual CAN interface using SocketCAN [5], a set of open source CAN drivers. The attack phase was simulated

---

[1] https://ocslab.hksecurity.net/Datasets/car-hacking-dataset.
[2] https://ocslab.hksecurity.net/Datasets/survival-ids.

Table 1. Overview of messages contained in the datasets.

KIA Soul	Number of messages	%
Flooding	Normal: 148,760	81.78
	Attack: 33,141	18.22
Fuzzy	Normal: 210,178	84.07
	Attack: 39,812	15.93
Malfunction	Normal: 166,035	95.73
	Attack: 7, 401	4.27

(b) Kia Soul dataset.

Car-Hacking	Number of messages	%
DoS	Normal: 3,078,250	83.97
	Attack: 587,521	16.03
Fuzzy	Normal: 3,347,013	87.19
	Attack: 491,847	12.81
Spoofing Gear	Normal: 3,845,890	86.56
	Attack: 597,252	13.44
Spoofing RPM	Normal: 3,966,805	85.83
	Attack: 654,897	14.17

(a) Car-Hacking dataset.

SA-Hacking	Number of messages	%
Fabrication	Normal: 1,322,823	82.82
	Attack: 274,400	17.18

(c) SA-Hacking dataset.

on the basis of the fabrication attack of Cho and Shin [19]. Six threads generate genuine data regarding the aforementioned bullet list of messages. Instead, a thread is used to generate attack messages. The WHEEL_SPEED (vehicle speed) and the STEER (steering angle) messages are chosen to create the fabrication attack. Every 10 s, 100 injected messages are sent without using the sleep function. Furthermore, each of these 100 messages is generated randomly using the *random* function[3]. Table 1(c) shows the normal and attack messages generated in about three hours. Values are saved into a Comma Separated Values (CSV) file with attributes: Timestamp, CAN DEC (the CAN ID in decimal form), CAN ID (the CAN ID in hexadecimal form), DLC, DATA, and flag. In the Generated Dataset, the value of the attribute Flag is 0 for normal messages and 1 for the fabrication attack messages.

5 Proposed Approach

5.1 Experimental Phase

MaREA[4] was tested with two different approaches. The first approach consists of validating MaREA with [22,25] that performed a multiclass classification with the Random Forest using the Car-Hacking Dataset to prove that our system outperformed the identified works in the literature.

In the second approach, to evaluate MaREA with a new type of attack and determine whether it is better than the classifier being analyzed, the Survival Analysis Dataset and the SA Hacking Dataset were concatenated to obtain a new dataset (Table 2(b)). The results obtained from MaREA were compared with [24], where the authors evaluated long-term memory (LSTM) for multiclass classification using the Survival Analysis Dataset.

---

[3] https://docs.python.org/3/library/os.html.
[4] https://github.com/SERLABUniba/MaREA.

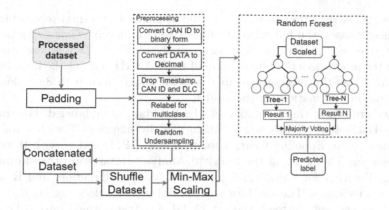

Fig. 1. An overview of the proposed methodology.

Table 2. Number of messages after the under-sampling is performed.

Label	Number messages	%	Label	Number messages	%
Normal	2,331,517	50.00	Normal	354,754	50.00
DoS	587,521	12.60	Flooding	33,141	4.67
Fuzzy	491,847	10.55	Fuzzy	39,812	5.61
Spoofing Gear	597,252	12.81	Malfunction	7,401	1.04
Spoofing RPM	654,897	14.04	Fabrication	274,400	38.67
(a) Under-sampling Car-Hacking dataset.			(b) Under-sampling Concatenated dataset.		

5.2 Experimental Setting

All the experiments were carried out on an Intel Core i7-11800H processor with 32 GB of RAM using Python 3 and the Scikit-learn library [33].

A Random Forest classifier [16] was used consisting of N decision trees, each of which will predict a class with majority vote. The class with the most votes becomes the model's prediction. Figure 1 shows an overview of the proposed methodology. The processed data set consists of the Car-Hacking, Survival Analysis, and SA-Hacking data set, where each of them is considered and processed individually. The padding process adds a '00' value at the end of the DATA attribute to remove any "Not a Number" (NaN) entries since all DATA attributes do not have a length of eight bytes. The padding algorithm takes the value contained in the DLC attribute and, if less than eight, adds the '00' values until it does not reach the length of eight. For example, if the DLC is four, to reach the length of eight, the algorithm will add '00' in the attribute from D4 to D7.

After padding, the preprocessing phase is performed, where the CAN IDs are transformed from hexadecimal to binary representation, obtaining eleven features. To clarify, the binary representation indicates that each CAN ID is first converted from hexadecimal to decimal form and then transformed into 0 and 1 because, for the standard identifier, it is a fixed 11-bit binary value. The

DATA features were transformed from hexadecimal to decimal representation. After these phases, the following attributes were removed: *Timestamp* because MaREA does not perform a time series analysis; *CAN ID* was also removed because the model uses the binary form of the CAN ID and not the hexadecimal values; *DLC*, as the features are in a specific range from 0 to 8, it does not provide useful information for the model.

As we are conducting a multiclass, the flag data are relabeled. For the Car Hacking Dataset, the labels were transformed by mapping T with 1 for DoS, 2 for Fuzzy, 3 for Spoofing Gear, 4 for Spoofing RPM, and R with 0 for normal messages. The labels of the Survival Analysis Dataset are transformed by mapping T with 1 for Flooding, 2 for Fuzzy, 3 for Malfunction, and R with 0 for Normal messages. The label for the normal message does not change in the SA-Hacking Dataset. Instead, the attack label is transformed into 4. For each dataset, a random under-sampling was performed to resolve the class imbalance, and finally, all processed datasets were concatenated. Table 2(a) shows the number of messages after undersampling for the Car Hacking data set, and Table 2 (b) shows the number of messages after undersampling for the concatenated Survival Analysis Dataset and the SA-Hacking Dataset. Before scaling the features, the examples are shuffled to ensure that the model does not learn any unintended pattern from the order of the data. Finally, since the features are not in a specific range, they are scaled in a range of $[0, 1]$ using the MinMaxScaler function[5]. The hyperparameters of the RF were evaluated using a grid search method by considering every combination of the values. Grid search was performed with 5-fold cross-validation using GridSearchCV[6]. Table 3 shows the values considered for the hyperparameters tuning for MaREA considering all datasets and the selected values for the Car-Hacking and Concatenated datasets.

After hyperparameters were adjusted, the concatenated data set was split into 70% for the train and 30% for the test.

Table 3. Hyperparameters considered and the values selected by the grid search for MaREA considering the Car-Hacking and Concatenated dataset.

Hyperparameters	Considered	Car-Hacking dataset	Concatenated dataset
n_estimators	9, 20, 50, 100	9	100
max_features	sqrt, log2, None	sqrt	sqrt
max_depth	10, 15, 20,25, 30, 40, None	20	40
min_samples_split	2, 5, 10	2	5
min_samples_leaf	1, 2, 4	1	1

---

[5] https://scikit-learn.org/stable/modules/generated/sklearn.preprocessing.MinMaxScaler.html.

[6] https://scikit-learn.org/stable/modules/generated/sklearn.model_selection.GridSearchCV.html.

Table 4. Comparison with other approaches that use Random Forest and the Car-Hacking Dataset as a testbed.

Reference	Accuracy	Precision	Recall	F1-Score
[22]	0.94	0.93	0.93	0.93
[25]	0.97	0.90	0.99	0.94
MaREA	0.99	0.99	0.99	0.99

Table 5. Comparison with a multi-class approach using the Survival Analysis Dataset as a testbed. The fabrication attack is reported only for MaREA. The precision score is not included in [24].

Reference	Model	Label	Accuracy %	Precision %	Recall %	F1-Score %
[24]	LSTM	Normal	0.9971	N/A	1.0	0.9994
		Flooding		N/A	1.0	1.0
		Fuzzy		N/A	0.9469	0.9701
		Malfunction		N/A	0.9697	0.9087
MaREA	Random Forest	Normal	0.9997	0.9999	1.0	0.9999
		Flooding		1.0	1.0	1.0
		Fuzzy		1.0	0.9956	0.9978
		Malfunction		0.9959	1.0	0.9979
		Fabrication		0.9994	1.0	0.9997

5.3 Evaluation Results

Precision, recall, F1 score, and accuracy metrics were used to compare the results. Table 4 shows the results using the Car-Hacking dataset. We can see that MaREA outperforms [22,25] in terms of the aforementioned metrics using a different pre-processing phase. With [25], MaREA obtains similar recall values.

Table 5 shows the results comparing MaREA with [24] using the Survival Analysis Dataset. Our model outperformed the LSTM model proposed by [24] for all types; normal, flood, fuzzy, and malfunction messages. However, both models obtained the same results for the flooding attacks, probably because the attack pattern for the flooding is easy to identify. MaREA obtained the best results for the Fuzzy and Malfunction attacks for the Recall and F1-Score metrics. In particular, the fuzzy attack is the most challenging, as the CAN IDs are randomly generated. Moreover, since MaREA is also trained with the combination of the Survival Analysis Dataset and the Synthetic Automotive Dataset, we can argue that the model generalizes properly by obtaining a low misclassification. The proposed preprocessing phase was proved to be robust in identifying CAN attacks.

6   Conclusion

This paper proposed a new synthetic automotive data set using a DBC file that can be used to generate new types of attack and an IDS called MaREA (Multi-Class Random Forest for Automotive Intrusion Detection). In the first experimental approach, MaREA was validated with two studies that used a random forest in a multiclass approach with the Car-Hacking Dataset as a testbed. Our approach achieved better results than the two random forest models. So, Random Forest was chosen as it is computationally less expansive than other Deep Learning algorithms. In the second experiment, MaREA was trained on another data set created by concatenating the Survival Analysis Dataset and the Synthetic Automotive Dataset. In this phase, the results were compared with an LSTM, where MaREA again achieved better results. In future work, we plan to create new attacks using the proposed DBC file and test the Synthetic Automotive Dataset with other models like state-of-the-art machine learning and deep learning algorithms.

Acknowledgments. This study has been partially supported by the following projects: SSA (Secure Safe Apulia, Codice Progetto 6ESURE5) and KEIRETSU (Codice Progetto V9UFIL5) funded by "Regolamento regionale della Puglia per gli aiuti in esenzione n. 17 December 2014 (BURP n. 139 suppl. del 06/10/2014) TITOLO II CAPO 1 DEL REGOLAMENTO GENERALE "Avviso per la presentazione dei progetti promossi da Grandi Imprese ai sensi dell'articolo 17 del Regolamento"; SERICS (PE00000014) under the MUR National Recovery and Resilience Plan funded by the European Union - NextGenerationEU.

References

1. Experimental Security Assessment of Mercedes-Benz Cars. https://keenlab. tencent.com/en/2021/05/12/Tencent-Security-Keen-Lab-Experimental-Security-Assessment-on-Mercedes-Benz-Cars/. Accessed 02 Mar 2022
2. Experimental Security Assessment on Lexus Cars. https://keenlab.tencent.com/en/2020/03/30/Tencent-Keen-Security-Lab-Experimental-Security-Assessment-on-Lexus-Cars/. Accessed 02 Mar 2022
3. Experimental Security Research of Tesla Autopilot. https://keenlab.tencent.com/en/2019/03/29/Tencent-Keen-Security-Lab-Experimental-Security-Research-of-Tesla-Autopilot/. Accessed 02 Mar 2022
4. Exploiting Wi-Fi Stack on Tesla Model S. https://keenlab.tencent.com/en/2020/01/02/exploiting-wifi-stack-on-tesla-model-s/. Accessed 02 Mar 2022
5. Socketcan - Controller Area network. https://docs.kernel.org/networking/can.html. Accessed 01 Mar 2022
6. Alfardus, A., Rawat, D.B.: Intrusion detection system for can bus in-vehicle network based on machine learning algorithms. In: 2021 IEEE 12th Annual Ubiquitous Computing, Electronics & Mobile Communication Conference (UEMCON), pp. 0944–0949. IEEE (2021)
7. Baldassarre, M.T., Barletta, V.S., Caivano, D.: Smart program management in a smart city. In: 2018 AEIT International Annual Conference. pp. 1–6 (2018). https://doi.org/10.23919/AEIT.2018.8577379

8. Baldassarre, M.T., Barletta, V.S., Caivano, D., Piccinno, A.: A visual tool for supporting decision-making in privacy oriented software development. In: Proceedings of the International Conference on Advanced Visual Interfaces. AVI 2020, Association for Computing Machinery, New York, NY, USA (2020). https://doi.org/10.1145/3399715.3399818

9. Baldassarre, M.T., Barletta, V.S., Caivano, D., Piccinno, A.: Integrating security and privacy in HCD-scrum. In: CHItaly 2021: 14th Biannual Conference of the Italian SIGCHI Chapter. CHItaly 2021, Association for Computing Machinery, New York, NY, USA (2021). https://doi.org/10.1145/3464385.3464746

10. Barletta, V.S., Caivano, D., Catalano, C., De Vincentiis, M., Pal, A.: Machine learning for automotive security in technology transfer. In: Information Systems and Technologies - WorldCIST 2023 (2023)

11. Barletta, V.S., Caivano, D., Nannavecchia, A., Scalera, M.: Intrusion detection for in-vehicle communication networks: an unsupervised Kohonen SOM approach. Future Internet 12(7), 119 (2020). https://doi.org/10.3390/fi12070119

12. Barletta, V.S., Caivano, D., Vincentiis, M.D., Ragone, A., Scalera, M., Martín, M.Á.S.: V-soc4as: a vehicle-soc for improving automotive security. Algorithms 16(2), 112 (2023). https://doi.org/10.3390/a16020112

13. Barletta, V.S., Cassano, F., Pagano, A., Piccinno, A.: New perspectives for cyber security in software development: when end-user development meets artificial intelligence. In: 2022 International Conference on Innovation and Intelligence for Informatics, Computing, and Technologies (3ICT), pp. 531–534. IEEE (2022)

14. Bosch: CAN Specification Version 2.0. Robert Bosch GmbH, Postfach 50 (1991)

15. Bozdal, M., Samie, M., Aslam, S., Jennions, I.: Evaluation of can bus security challenges. Sensors 20(8), 2364 (2020)

16. Breiman, L.: Random forests 45(1), 5–32 (2001)

17. Buscemi, A., Turcanu, I., Castignani, G., Crunelle, R., Engel, T.: CANmatch: a fully automated tool for can bus reverse engineering based on frame matching. IEEE Trans. Veh. Technol. 70(12), 12358–12373 (2021)

18. Catalano, C., Afrune, P., Angelelli, M., Maglio, G., Striani, F., Tommasi, F.: Security testing reuse enhancing active cyber defence in public administration. In: ITASEC, pp. 120–132 (2021)

19. Cho, K.T., Shin, K.G.: Fingerprinting electronic control units for vehicle intrusion detection. In: USENIX Security Symposium, vol. 40, pp. 911–27 (2016)

20. De Vincentiis, M., Cassano, F., Pagano, A., Piccinno, A.: QAI4ASE: quantum artificial intelligence for automotive software engineering. In: Proceedings of the 1st International Workshop on Quantum Programming for Software Engineering, pp. 19–21. QP4SE 2022, Association for Computing Machinery, New York, NY, USA (2022)

21. El-Rewini, Z., Sadatsharan, K., Selvaraj, D.F., Plathottam, S.J., Ranganathan, P.: Cybersecurity challenges in vehicular communications. Veh. Commun. 23, 100214 (2020)

22. Gundu, R., Maleki, M.: Securing CAN bus in connected and autonomous vehicles using supervised machine learning approaches. In: 2022 IEEE International Conference on Electro Information Technology (EIT), pp. 042–046. IEEE (2022)

23. Han, M.L., Kwak, B.I., Kim, H.K.: Anomaly intrusion detection method for vehicular networks based on survival analysis. Veh. Commun. 14, 52–63 (2018)

24. Hossain, M.D., Inoue, H., Ochiai, H., Fall, D., Kadobayashi, Y.: LSTM-based intrusion detection system for in-vehicle can bus communications. IEEE Access 8, 185489–185502 (2020)

25. Kalkan, S.C., Sahingoz, O.K.: In-vehicle intrusion detection system on controller area network with machine learning models. In: 2020 11th International Conference on Computing, Communication and Networking Technologies (ICCCNT), pp. 1–6 (2020)
26. Kim, K., Kim, J.S., Jeong, S., Park, J.H., Kim, H.K.: Cybersecurity for autonomous vehicles: review of attacks and defense. Comput. Secur. **103**, 102150 (2021)
27. Marchetti, M., Stabili, D.: READ: reverse engineering of automotive data frames. IEEE Trans. Inf. Forensics Secur. **14**(4), 1083–1097 (2019)
28. Martínez-Cruz, A., Ramírez-Gutiérrez, K.A., Feregrino-Uribe, C., Morales-Reyes, A.: Security on in-vehicle communication protocols: issues, challenges, and future research directions. Comput. Commun. **180**, 1–20 (2021)
29. Miller, C., Valasek, C.: Adventures in automotive networks and control units. Def Con **21**(260–264), 15–31 (2013)
30. Miller, C., Valasek, C.: Remote exploitation of an unaltered passenger vehicle. Black Hat USA **2015**(S 91), 1–91 (2015)
31. Moulahi, T., Zidi, S., Alabdulatif, A., Atiquzzaman, M.: Comparative performance evaluation of intrusion detection based on machine learning in in-vehicle controller area network bus. IEEE Access **9**, 99595–99605 (2021)
32. NVIDIA: Jetson AGX Xavier Series. https://www.nvidia.com/en-us/autonomous-machines/embedded-systems/jetson-agx-xavier/. Accessed 25 Jul 2023
33. Pedregosa, F., et al.: Scikit-learn: machine learning in Python. J. Mach. Learn. Res. **12**, 2825–2830 (2011)
34. Rajapaksha, S., Kalutarage, H., Al-Kadri, M.O., Petrovski, A., Madzudzo, G., Cheah, M.: Ai-based intrusion detection systems for in-vehicle networks: a survey. ACM Comput. Surv. **55**(11), 1–40 (2023)
35. Seo, E., Song, H.M., Kim, H.K.: GIDS: gan based intrusion detection system for in-vehicle network. In: 2018 16th Annual Conference on Privacy, Security and Trust (PST), pp. 1–6 (2018)
36. Serrano, M.A., et al.: Minimizing incident response time in real-world scenarios using quantum computing. Softw. Qual. J. 1–30 (2023). https://doi.org/10.1007/s11219-023-09632-6
37. Song, H.M., Woo, J., Kim, H.K.: In-vehicle network intrusion detection using deep convolutional neural network. Veh. Commun. **21**, 100198 (2020)
38. Stabili, D., Ferretti, L., Andreolini, M., Marchetti, M.: DAGA: detecting attacks to in-vehicle networks via n-gram analysis. IEEE Trans. Veh. Technol. **71**(11), 11540–11554 (2022)
39. Venturi, A., Stabili, D., Pollicino, F., Bianchi, E., Marchetti, M.: Comparison of machine learning-based anomaly detectors for controller area network. In: 2022 IEEE 21st International Symposium on Network Computing and Applications (NCA), vol. 21, pp. 81–88. IEEE (2022)
40. Yang, L., Moubayed, A., Hamieh, I., Shami, A.: Tree-based intelligent intrusion detection system in internet of vehicles. In: 2019 IEEE Global Communications Conference (GLOBECOM), pp. 1–6. IEEE (2019)

Forecasting the Developer's Impact in Managing the Technical Debt

Lerina Aversano[1][iD], Mario Luca Bernardi[1][iD], Marta Cimitile[2][iD], and Martina Iammarino[1][✉][iD]

[1] Department of Engineering, University of Sannio, Benevento, Italy
{aversano,bernardi,iammarino}@unisannio.it
[2] UnitelmaSapienza University, Rome, Italy
marta.cimitile@unitelmasapienza.it

Abstract. Technical debt is a collection of design decisions that, when taken together over time, make the system challenging to maintain and develop. Technical debt impacts the quality of applications by generating structural weaknesses that translate into slowness and functional deficiencies at the development level. Identifying debts in your code, architecture, and infrastructure is of paramount importance and requires an in-depth analysis that requires effort in terms of time and resources. To date, there are several reliable tools for calculating debt in code, but this study aims to forecast the impact developers have on debt in source code. We propose an approach, based on the use of different Machine Learning and Deep Learning classifiers capable of predicting just in time, if the change that the developer is making will have a low, medium, or high impact on the debt. To conduct the experiments, three open-source Java systems available on Github were selected, and for each of these, the entire history was collected in terms of changes, quality metrics and indicators strictly connected to the presence of technical debt. The results obtained are satisfactory, showing the effectiveness of the proposed method.

Keywords: Technical Debt · Developer's Impact · Machine Learning · Deep Learning

1 Introduction

The term Technical Debt (TD) refers to the consequences of software development actions that intentionally or unintentionally prioritize customer value on the one hand and project obligations on the other over more in-depth technical considerations and implementations. Simply put, this is written code that will take more man-hours to fix. Cunningham proposed the concept of "technical debt" as a metaphor to explain the effects of development shortcuts and potential project issues that may arise if proper measures are not taken to maintain the highest quality overall solution [9]. It shows how much it will cost to rework a solution after selecting a simple but ineffective one.

© The Author(s), under exclusive license to Springer Nature Switzerland AG 2024
R. Kadgien et al. (Eds.): PROFES 2023, LNCS 14484, pp. 35–47, 2024.
https://doi.org/10.1007/978-3-031-49269-3_4

The accumulation of debt is not due to writing bad quality code but to the dynamics of software projects where there may be a misalignment between the work of the development team and the needs of the business. Therefore, to avoid the accumulation of debt, it is necessary to systematically subject the code to a refactoring action. The term "debt" is not accidental: over the years, the interest has increased, in the sense that it is increasingly difficult to get your hands on the code and modernize it. The functionality of the code is compromised when TD is introduced, which lowers the overall quality of the code. Although the software may still function, the bugs in the code must be corrected before it can perform to its maximum potential [11]. The biggest issue with TD in the code is that, like many debts, if it is not paid off, it may accrue interest, which might seriously harm the project's ability to be completed on time and with high quality [10,24]. Therefore, the reduction of the TD must start above all from understanding its origin and from analyzing the metrics to plan the work. To date, numerous studies have focused on the study of TD and its management. The TD and its administration have been comprehensively mapped by Li et al. [15]. Yli-Huumo et al. [22] looked into how software development teams actually deal with technical debt. Others have concentrated on the investigation of Self Admitted Technical Debt (SATD), a specific sort of TD in which developers acknowledge they are adding debt to the code by disclosing it in the supporting comments [4].

Similarly, several tools for detecting TD have been developed [1,14], but evaluating TD might not be enough to prevent a software system's quality from being completely compromised, so other studies have focused on predicting future value because it could be of great help as it would facilitate development and maintenance. Therefore, on the basis of what is already present in the literature, this study aims to explore a still open research question, investigating the role of developers in TD management. The goal of this study is to predict whether developing has a positive or negative impact on TD.

Three open-source software systems were selected to conduct the study, for which the entire history was considered, commit by commit. For each system, various process parameters were collected, some relating to quality and others strictly connected to the presence of TD. For each commit, the committer has been identified, and using metrics gathered for earlier commits, we aim to predict the developer's impact on the TD before the commit is even modified. To make the prediction we used both Machine Learning and Deep Learning methods, to understand which model best suited our case.

This paper is structured as follows. A brief summary of related work is presented in Sect. 2. The proposed approach is described in Sect. 3, while the experiment results are discussed in Sect. 4. Finally, in Sect. 5 the conclusions and future works are reported.

2   Related Works

TD is a metaphor introduced to represent the effort required to fix defects that remain in the code when an application is released. It can be seen as the difference, in terms of bugs, between what is expected and what is delivered.

Detecting the TD is important because its presence could compromise the quality of the software system, and for that matter, there are several tools capable of identifying the TD in the source code, such as Teamscale[1], Ndepend[2], or Cast[3]. The most used, according to a recent research is Sonarqube [6], which provides the value in time/person, necessary to calculate the TD. It is based on the Software Quality Assessment Based on Lifecycle Expectations (SQALE) approach. Using this method, it is feasible to pinpoint the software system components that create debt in the code, assess the effects on qualitative traits, and calculate the expense of fixing the debt-causing factors.

To date, numerous studies have focused on the identification of TD [15], on the impact this has on code quality metrics [5,21], on the importance of the particular type of self-admitted TD [12,13], and above all on the possibility of prediction [3,19,20]. For example, in the study [2], the authors focused on the just-in-time prediction of the TD trend, because the developer, knowing the effects of the modification he is making, could be directed to make improvements, thus avoiding the deterioration of the code. The approach was based on a Deep Learning model, validated on a large data set of Open Source Java systems.

Just as it is important to predict the value of the TD or its trend, it is also very important to understand the role that developers have. In order to comprehend how ownership and alignment of contributions affect the buildup of technical code debt and how sudden changes in team composition affect a team's ability to manage TD, Zabardast et al. have conducted an interesting study [23]. The findings imply that alignment of contributions may be crucial in preventing TD in software development companies. Organizations can reduce the dependence across teams and hold teams accountable for the quality of the components they have the greatest experience with.

To the best of our knowledge, no studies have aimed to predict the impact a developer has on code with a given change. In this regard, this study explores an approach capable of predicting, simultaneously with the modification that is being made to the code, whether the developer's impact on TD will be low, medium, or high, given the trend of some characterizing metrics such as those of quality and those strictly connected to the presence of TD.

3   Approach

In this section, we describe the proposed approach to perform a developer impact prediction on TD in software systems. More in detail, in the following subsections

---

[1] https://www.cqse.eu/en/teamscale/overview/.
[2] https://www.ndepend.com.
[3] https://www.castsoftware.com.

we provide detailed information on the data used, on the proposed feature model, and on the main tasks underlying our approach, the data extraction task, the calculation of the author's impact on the TD trend, and on the prediction one.

3.1   Dataset

To conduct the experiments, the dataset was built by selecting 3 open-source Java software systems, all available on GitHub. The main characteristics of these systems are reported in Table 1. The first column lists the names of the projects, the second column lists the label by which we will refer to them, the third column lists the number of classes that are thought to be affected by TD, the fourth column lists the number of commits, and the last column lists the time period to which the analyzed commits belong.

Table 1. Software Systems characteristics

Name	ID	N. classes	N. commit	Commit Time-laps
Jackson-dataformat-xml	JDF	336	1406	30 December 2010 — 1 October 2020
Commons-imaging	CIM	1568	1334	12 October 2007 — 31 August 2020
Javassist	JAV	545	944	22 April 2003 — 21 September 2021

3.2   Features Model

For each system, a large model of features was extracted, based on all product metrics. Specifically, measures purely related to the existence of TD in the code as well as metrics relating to the product quality of the software were extracted.

With the latter, the TD is found by examining the artifacts created throughout the course of the software's life cycle. The results of the source code analysis, in particular the TD metrics, show the presence of any defects, vulnerabilities, or violations of sound programming practices that lead to errors or lower the product's quality. We especially find code smells among them, which, according to Alves et al. [1] and Palomba et al. [17], are signs of bad design and implementation choices that can harm the code's readability and maintainability. These indicators are beneficial since they show that refactoring is required. These metrics are shown in Table 2.

Instead, as regards the metrics relating to the quality of the source code, fundamental indicators for the presence of TD, we have considered the object-oriented quality metrics in the model. These metrics provide a prospective assessment of the long-term maintainability of various system properties. In particular, the cohesion, complexity, size, and coupling of the code are evaluated using the metrics previously specified by Chidaber and Kemerer [8] and other quantitative metrics. If these factors are not managed appropriately, the TD increases. These metrics are shown in Table 3.

Table 2. TD indicator metrics

Indicator	Description
Bugs	Total of bugs
Functions	Java only counts the methods that are part of the classes, omitting any that are part of anonymous classes
Code smells	Number of source code smells overall
Classes	Total number of classes (including all subtypes such as interfaces, enumerations, and nested classes)
Complexity	The cyclomatic difficulty of a specific section of code is determined by the number of linearly unique pathways through the source code. If there are no decision points in the source code, such as IF or FOR loops, the complexity will be 1. If the code comprises a single IF with a single condition, there will be two alternative pathways
Comment lines	Total sum of lines containing comments and commented code. Blank lines or lines with only special characters are not taken into account
Comment lines density	Comment line density = Comment lines/(Code lines + Comment lines) * 100 With such a formula, values equal to: a) 50% mean that the number of lines of code equals the number of comment lines b) 100% indicates that the file contains only comment lines
Vulnerabilities	Amount of vulnerabilities
Cognitive complexity	Assessment of how difficult it is to comprehend control flow
Ncloc	Number of lines of code not commented
Sqale index	Represents the exact value of the TD in the source code
Sqale rating	Shows the grade given to the technical debt ratio. There are several intervals in it: A = 0–0.05, B = 0.06–0.1, C = 0.11–0.20, D = 0.21–0.5, E = 0.51+-1
Sqale debt ratio	Remediation cost/Development cost, which can be expressed as: Remediation cost/(Cost for developing 1 line of code * Total of lines of code). Ratio of the cost of developing the software to the cost of repairing it
Nominal Delta	Indicates the progress of the TD in the code of a specific Java class between a commit and its previous one Takes the value *stable* when there is no change in the TD, *increase* when there is an increase and *decrease* when there is a decrease in the value of the TD compared to the previous commit

3.3 Data Extraction Task

Five steps were performed to extract and collect features.

Using GIT commands, the change history for each software system was recovered during the first phase. The source code for each class of each software system was examined commit by commit in the second phase to assess how it had changed over time. The SonarQube[4] and CK[5] tools were specially employed. The first is an open-source tool to assist developers that ensures continuous code inspection and offers hundreds of automated criteria for static code analysis. It is used to detect the metrics indicating the presence of the TD and its value. On more than 20 programming languages, this can identify errors, code smells, and security problems. The second tool, which is used to compute code quality metrics, uses static analysis rather than compiled code to determine class and method-level metrics in Java projects. In the third phase, for each analyzed commit the authors were extracted. In the fourth phase, all the extracted data for each software system has been combined into a single dataset that contains the history of commit changes for each Java class taken into consideration. In the last

---

[4] https://www.sonarsource.com/products/sonarqube.
[5] https://github.com/mauricioaniche/ck.

Table 3. Product metrics - Quality Indicators

Indicator	Description
Lack of Cohesion of Methods	The ability of a method to only access class characteristics is expressed by the cohesiveness of the method. Due to the existence of various methods to access similar properties, there is a lack of cohesiveness
Depth of Inheritance Tree	Maximum separation between a node (a class) and the tree's root, which represents the hereditary structure. The number of methods a class can inherit increases with the depth of the hierarchy
Weight Method Count per Class	Weighted sum of a class's methods, where each method's weight is determined by a factor of your choosing for method complexity
Coupling Between Objects	Number of collaborations of a class, that is, the number of other classes to which it is coupled
Response For a Class	The 'volume' of interaction between classes is indicated. High values result in an increase in the class's design complexity and testing effort
Non-Commented, non-empty Lines of Code	Number of lines of code, except of orblank lines
Number of methods	Total amount of methods: static, public, abstract, private, protected, predefined, final, and synchronized
Number of static invocation	Amount of calls made to static methods overall
Number of unique words	Count of unique words
Parenthesized expressions	Count of expressions in parentheses
Number of fields	Number of set of fields: static, public, private, protected, default, final, and synchronized
Comparisons	Count of comparisons (e.g. == or !=)
Returns	Total of return statements
Try/catches	Count of try and catches
Number	Quantity of numbers (i.e. int, long, double, float)
Loops	Count of loops statements (while, for, do while, generalized for)
Variables	Numerical index of variables declared
Math Operations	Count of mathematical operations (divisions, remainder, plus, minus, right and left shift)
String literals	how many string literals there are (like "John Doe"). The number of times that repeated strings appear is counted
Anonymous classes, subclasses and lambda expressions	Number of anonymous declarations of classes or subclasses
Usage of each field	Determine how much of each field is used in each method
Max nested blocks	The highest number of blocks nested together
Usage of each variable	Calculate the usage of each variable in each method
Modifiers	Number of public/abstract/private/protected/native modifiers of classes/methods

phase, the data underwent cleaning, normalization, and balancing. In particular, as regards the latter, the datasets of the three systems analyzed showed a strong imbalance in the stable class, the one in which the value of the TD remained unchanged in a class between the commit and its predecessor. In this regard, stratified undersampling was used, which consists of eliminating some observations from the most populated class. More specifically, stratified undersampling takes the observations more carefully, trying to maintain the proportions of the original dataset for one or more variables.

3.4 Developer's Impact Calculation Task

In this phase, the impact this has on the trend of the TD was calculated for each author present in the dataset. More specifically, a new feature has been created, which will be our target variable in the classification task. Based on the trend of the extracted metrics, indicators of the quality of the code, and the presence of the TD, a special function was created in Python, capable of evaluating the impact of the modifications of a specific author. More specifically, the function calculates the impact value based on the nominal delta variable, which indicates whether, in a specific commit compared to the previous one, the TD value has remained unchanged (stable), increased (increase), or decreased (decrease). Finally, the function returns a value, an impact indicator, which is the average impact of all the changes made by the author in a specific software system. Finally, three thresholds have been defined to evaluate the impact. The impact was defined as low when the index was between 0.0 and 0.3, medium between 0.31 and 0.6, and high between 0.61 and 1. Therefore our target variable can take on three values: low, medium, and high.

3.5 Forecasting Task

Two types of classifiers were used to predict the impact of developers on TD trends. On the one hand, Machine Learning classifiers were used, such as Decision Tree (DT), Random Forest(RF), and K-nearest Neighbor (KNN), on the other, a Deep Learning model based on a Long Short Term Memory (LSTM) network was used.

In DT learning from a tree is done by dividing the source into subsets based on a value attribution test. This process is repeated on each derived subset, following a recursive pattern [18]. RF represents an aggregate of independent decision trees, which do not influence each other [16]. These are trained with a subset of the randomly generated training data frame. The KNN is a non-parametric supervised learning classifier, which uses proximity to make classifications or predictions about the clustering of a single data point [25]. LSTMs are one of the architectures studied starting from recurrent neural networks (RNN). One of the main advantages of LSTMs is the ability to learn from long-time sequences and retain their memory. Specifically, the LSTM was built through the use of three Dense layers, using the softmax as the activation function of the last layers.

Hyperparameter optimization was applied to each classifier, through the GridSeaarch library, to find the best possible configuration. Grid search is a technique used in machine learning to find the best hyperparameters of a model and consists of defining a grid of values for each hyperparameter and testing all possible combinations of values. Specifically for the Decision Tree classifier, the following parameters have been optimized, with the following values:

- max-depth : The maximum depth of the tree. The chosen values could vary between 'None',5, 10, and 20.
- min_samples_leaf: The minimum number of samples required to be at a leaf node. The values could vary between 2, 5, 10, 20.

– min_samples_split: The minimum number of samples required to split an internal node. The values could vary between 1, 2, 4, 8.

For the K-nearest neighbors classifier, the following parameters have been optimized, with the following values:

– n_neighbors: Number of neighbors. The values could vary between 3, 5, and 7.
– weights: Weight function used in prediction. The values it can take are 'uniform', or 'distance'. In the first case, All points in each neighborhood are weighted equally. In the second case, closer neighbors of a query point will have a greater influence than neighbors which are further away.
– 'metric': Metric to use for distance computation. The values it can take are 'euclidean' or 'manhattan'.

The following parameters have been optimized for the Random Forest classifier, with the following values:

– n_estimators: Represents the number of trees in the forest. The values
– it can vary from are 100, 200, 300.
– max_depth: The values it can vary from are None, 5, 10, 20.
– min_samples_split: The values it can vary from are 2, 5, 10, 20.
– min_samples_leaf: The values it can vary between are 1, 2, 4, and 8.

Finally, for the Long Short Term Memory, we decided to optimize the following parameters, with the following values:

– batch_size: The number of samples contained in each batch. It can take the value 32 or 64.
– epochs: It can take a value of 25 or 50.
– units: Positive integer, the dimensionality of the output space. It can take the value 64 or 128.
– dropout : Can take the value 0.2 or 0.4.

To validate the models, Cross Validation [7] was used, which divides the initial dataset into a series of equal portions of data and iteratively uses k-1 for the train and 1 for the test. The performance of these classifiers was compared to understand which model best suited our data. In particular, the validation metrics, accuracy, precision, recall, and F-score, which represent the harmonic mean of precision and recall, F_1, were used to evaluate the accuracy of the model. Accuracy is the ratio of the number of correct predictions of an event to the total number of times the model predicts it, and recall measures the sensitivity of the model because it indicates the ratio of correct predictions for a class to the total number of cases in which it occurs.

4   Results

In this section, we report the results of the experiments conducted. For each classifier used we report a table with the performance of the model on all the software systems considered. More specifically, each table contains the best performance, obtained with the best hyperparameters. In the first column, there is the system ID, in the following columns the optimized parameters, and in the last four columns the model validation metrics calculated on the test: accuracy (A), precision (P), recall (R), and F1-score (F1).

Table 4 shows the best performances obtained with the Decision Tree classifier. For this, three parameters, max depth, min-samples-leaf, and min-samples-split were subjected to optimization. The results show that the performance of the Decision Tree in terms of F1-score varies between 92% and 99% in the case of JAV. In most cases, the max-depth is 20, min-samples-leaf 1 and min-samples-split 10.

Table 4. Results of Decision Tree

System	max-depth	min_samples_leaf	min_samples_split	A	P	R	F1
JAV	20	1	5	99.75	98.99	98.93	99.19
JDF	5	1	10	99.39	99.79	88.99	92.33
CIM	20	8	10	99.08	95.66	95.19	95.39

Table 5 shows the best performances obtained with the K-nearest neighbors classifier. The results show that the performance in terms of F1-score is excellent, ranging between 99% and 100% in the case of CIM. In most cases, the n_neighbors is equal to 3, while weights and metric are always equal to 'distance' and 'euclidean' respectively.

Table 5. Results of K-nearest neighbors

System	n_neighbors	weights	metric	A	P	R	F1
JAV	3	distance	euclidean	99.73	98.79	98.86	99.06
JDF	3	distance	euclidean	99.91	100	98.33	99.06
CIM	7	distance	euclidean	99.94	99.86	99.93	100

Table 6 shows the best performances obtained with the Random Forest classifier. The results show that the F1-score oscillates between 93% of JDF and 99% of JAV. As for the parameters, in most cases, the best performance is obtained with max_depth equal to None, n_estimator equal to 200, min_samples_leaf equal to 1, and min_samples_split equal to 10.

Table 7 shows the best performances obtained with the LSTM classifier. The results are good, but not at the level of previous classifiers. In this case, the F-score ranges between 76% and 90%.

Finally, Fig. 1 shows the graph that compares the performance of all the classifiers used in terms of F1-Score for each system analyzed. Specifically, the performance of the DT in blue, KNN in green, RF in gray, and LSTM in yellow.

Table 6. Results of Random Forest

System	max_depth	n_estimator	min_samples_leaf	min_samples_split	A	P	R	F1
JAV	20	100	2	1	98.78	99.06	99.13	99.19
JDF	None	200	1	10	99.77	94.86	93.93	92.99
CIM	None	200	1	10	98.78	99.06	98.39	98.99

On the abscissa axis, we find the three systems, while on the ordinate axis the value of F1. The graph shows that in general all classifiers perform well, and are therefore able to predict the developer's impact on TD in the source code. So, finally, out of the three systems, the classifier with the best performance is KNN, followed by RF, DT, and LSTM. It is possible to conclude that the chosen feature model allows the classifier to optimally predict the developer's impact on the TD.

Table 7. Results of Long Short Term Memory

System	batch_size	epochs	units	dropout_rate	A	P	R	F1
JAV	64	50	128	0.2	98.93	92.13	90.06	90.79
JDF	64	50	64	0.4	99.64	75.92	76.25	76.19
CIM	32	50	64	0.2	99.70	85.26	88.19	86.46

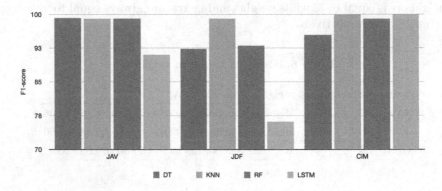

Fig. 1. Performance comparison of the classifiers in terms of F1-Score

5   Conclusions and Future Work

TD is the discrepancy between what has been completed and what would ideally be required in order to consider an action completed. The reason it is seen as a "debt" is because it shows a lack of regard for what was anticipated. Additionally, similar to many loans, if it is not paid back, interest may accrue and harm the enterprise as a whole. Because of this, TD has captured the curiosity of both academics and businesses.

In particular, this study focuses on the prediction of the impact that developers have on the TD present in the source code. We test and validate an approach based on the use of Machine Learning and Deep Learning techniques, capable of predicting at the same time with the change that the developer is making whether its impact will be low, medium, or high. Specifically, we use four classifiers: Random Forest, Decision Tree, K-nearest neighbors, and an LSTM network, and compare their results. The experiments were conducted on three open-source Java systems, Jackson Dataformat, Commons Imaging, and Javassit, for which we consider the entire evolutionary history in terms of modifications, quality metrics, and indicators closely related to the presence of TD.

The results are very encouraging and show the effectiveness of the proposed model. In particular, the classifier that best fits our research question is the K-nearest-neighbors, which obtains an F-score between 99% and 100% for all systems considered. Followed by the Decision Tree, Random Forest, and lastly the Deep Learning model. In fact, the LSTM seems to be the model that least fits the target.

In the future, it would be interesting to create a recommendation system for developers, based on this approach, which allows them to make the right change aware of the impact this will have on the source code, so as to prevent it from growing to such an extent as to compromise the functioning of the system.

References

1. Alves, N.S., Mendes, T.S., de Mendonça, M.G., Spínola, R.O., Shull, F., Seaman, C.: Identification and management of technical debt: a systematic mapping study. Inf. Softw. Technol. **70**, 100–121 (2016). https://doi.org/10.1016/j.infsof.2015.10.008. https://www.sciencedirect.com/science/article/abs/pii/S0950584915001743
2. Ardimento, P., Aversano, L., Bernardi, M.L., Cimitile, M., Iammarino, M.: Using deep temporal convolutional networks to just-in-time forecast technical debt principal. J. Syst. Softw. **194**, 111481 (2022). https://doi.org/10.1016/j.jss.2022.111481. https://www.sciencedirect.com/science/article/pii/S0164121222001649
3. Aversano, L., Bernardi, M.L., Cimitile, M., Iammarino, M., Montano, D.: Forecasting technical debt evolution in software systems: an empirical study. Front. Comp. Sci. **17**(3), 173210 (2023)
4. Aversano, L., Iammarino, M., Carapella, M., Vecchio, A.D., Nardi, L.: On the relationship between self-admitted technical debt removals and technical debt measures. Algorithms **13**(7), 168 (2020). https://www.mdpi.com/1999-4893/13/7/168
5. Aversano, L., Iammarino, M., Carapella, M., Vecchio, A.D., Nardi, L.: On the relationship between self-admitted technical debt removals and technical debt measures. Algorithms **13**(7) (2020). https://doi.org/10.3390/a13070168. https://www.mdpi.com/1999-4893/13/7/168
6. Avgeriou, P.C., et al.: An overview and comparison of technical debt measurement tools. IEEE Softw. **38**(3), 61–71 (2021). https://doi.org/10.1109/MS.2020.3024958
7. Browne, M.W.: Cross-validation methods. J. Math. Psychol. **44**(1), 108–132 (2000)
8. Chidamber, S.R., Kemerer, C.F.: A metrics suite for object oriented design. IEEE Trans. Softw. Eng. **20**(6), 476–493 (1994). https://doi.org/10.1109/32.295895

9. Cunningham, W.: The WyCash portfolio management system. In: Addendum to the Proceedings on Object-oriented Programming Systems, Languages, and Applications. ACM (1992)
10. Cunningham, W.: The wycash portfolio management system. SIGPLAN OOPS Mess 4(2), 29–30 (1992). https://doi.org/10.1145/157710.157715
11. Digkas, G., Ampatzoglou, A., Chatzigeorgiou, A., Avgeriou, P., Matei, O., Heb, R.: The risk of generating technical debt interest: a case study. SN Comput. Sci. 2, 12 (2021). https://doi.org/10.1007/s42979-020-00406-6
12. Iammarino, M., Zampetti, F., Aversano, L., Di Penta, M.: Self-admitted technical debt removal and refactoring actions: co-occurrence or more? In: 2019 IEEE International Conference on Software Maintenance and Evolution (ICSME), pp. 186–190 (2019). https://doi.org/10.1109/ICSME.2019.00029
13. Iammarino, M., Zampetti, F., Aversano, L., Di Penta, M.: An empirical study on the co-occurrence between refactoring actions and self-admitted technical debt removal. J. Syst. Softw. 178, 110976 (2021). https://doi.org/10.1016/j.jss.2021.110976. https://www.sciencedirect.com/science/article/pii/S016412122100073X
14. Letouzey, J.: The SQALE method for evaluating technical debt. In: 2012 Third International Workshop on Managing Technical Debt (MTD), pp. 31–36 (2012). https://doi.org/10.1109/MTD.2012.6225997
15. Li, Z., Avgeriou, P., Liang, P.: A systematic mapping study on technical debt and its management. J. Syst. Softw. 101, 193–220 (2015). https://doi.org/10.1016/j.jss.2014.12.027. https://www.sciencedirect.com/science/article/abs/pii/S0164121214002854
16. Liu, Y., Wang, Y., Zhang, J.: New machine learning algorithm: random forest. In: Liu, B., Ma, M., Chang, J. (eds.) ICICA 2012. LNCS, vol. 7473, pp. 246–252. Springer, Heidelberg (2012). https://doi.org/10.1007/978-3-642-34062-8_32
17. Palomba, F., Bavota, G., Di Penta, M., Fasano, F., Oliveto, R., De Lucia, A.: On the diffuseness and the impact on maintainability of code smells: A large scale empirical investigation. In: Proceedings of the 40th International Conference on Software Engineering, ICSE 2018, p. 482. Association for Computing Machinery, New York (2018). https://doi.org/10.1145/3180155.3182532
18. Rokach, L., Maimon, O.: Data Mining with Decision Trees. World Scientific, 2nd edn. (2014). https://doi.org/10.1142/9097. https://www.worldscientific.com/doi/abs/10.1142/9097
19. Tsoukalas, D., Jankovic, M., Siavvas, M., Kehagias, D., Chatzigeorgiou, A., Tzovaras, D.: On the applicability of time series models for technical debt forecasting. In: 15th China-Europe International Symposium on Software Engineering Education (2019)
20. Tsoukalas, D., Kehagias, D., Siavvas, M., Chatzigeorgiou, A.: Technical debt forecasting: an empirical study on open-source repositories. J. Syst. Softw. 170, 110777 (2020). https://doi.org/10.1016/j.jss.2020.110777. https://www.sciencedirect.com/science/article/pii/S0164121220301904
21. Wehaibi, S., Shihab, E., Guerrouj, L.: Examining the impact of self-admitted technical debt on software quality. In: 2016 IEEE 23rd International Conference on Software Analysis, Evolution, and Reengineering (SANER), vol. 1, pp. 179–188 (2016). https://doi.org/10.1109/SANER.2016.72
22. Yli-Huumo, J., Maglyas, A., Smolander, K.: How do software development teams manage technical debt? - an empirical study. J. Syst. Softw. 120, 195–218 (2016). https://doi.org/10.1016/j.jss.2016.05.018. https://www.sciencedirect.com/science/article/pii/S016412121630053X

23. Zabardast, E., Gonzalez-Huerta, J., Palma, F., Chatzipetrou, P.: The impact of ownership and contribution alignment on code technical debt accumulation. arXiv preprint arXiv:2304.02140 (2023)
24. Zazworka, N., Shaw, M.A., Shull, F., Seaman, C.: Investigating the impact of design debt on software quality. In: Proceedings of the 2nd Workshop on Managing Technical Debt, MTD 2011, pp. 17–23. Association for Computing Machinery, New York (2011). https://doi.org/10.1145/1985362.1985366
25. Zhang, Z.: Introduction to machine learning: k-nearest neighbors. Ann. Transl. Med. 4(11) (2016)

Development of a Desktop Application to Enable Doctors to Remotely Monitor Patients' Hematological Parameters

Mauro Giuseppe Camporeale[✉] [iD], Lucio Colizzi[iD], Nunzia Lomonte[iD], and Azzurra Ragone[iD]

Università degli Studi di Bari "Aldo Moro", Bari, Italy
mauro.camporeale@uniba.it

Abstract. The constant advancement of technology has revolutionized the healthcare industry, introducing new opportunities for improved medical services. Desktop applications have emerged as a versatile platform for enhancing healthcare delivery, providing efficient access to medical information and services. In this paper, we explore the development of a desktop application tailored specifically as a side application to a non-invasive anemia detection system, to allow patients and physicians to easily interact. By leveraging our expertise in software engineering principles and collaborating closely with medical experts, we present a comprehensive framework that incorporates advanced features, security protocols, and intuitive user interfaces, ensuring a reliable and secure desktop application that enables doctors to remotely monitor patients' hematological parameters extracted from the mobile application on the patients' smartphone.

Keywords: E-health · Software Engineering · Anemia Detection

1 Introduction

The healthcare industry faces unique challenges in adapting to the evolving digital landscape, where accessibility, efficiency, and accuracy are paramount [3,19]. As medical practitioners strive to deliver quality care to patients [20], software engineers play a crucial role in developing innovative solutions that harness the power of desktop applications. In this paper, we delve into the process of creating an application that caters specifically to medical service providers in the field of non-invasive anemia detection, empowering them to streamline their operations and enhance the overall patient-physician relationship.

Publications from the World Health Organization show that anemia is a widespread global health problem, affecting around 25% of people with varying degrees of severity [5]. In scientific writing, anemia is defined by a drop in red blood cells and hemoglobin levels, which results in less oxygen being transported to tissues and reduced blood function. Keeping close track of severe anemia is important because it can substantially cut the oxygen available to cells, negatively impacting vital organs. In this case, hemoglobin levels have to be often

R. Kadgien et al. (Eds.): PROFES 2023, LNCS 14484, pp. 48–59, 2024.
https://doi.org/10.1007/978-3-031-49269-3_5

measured by analyzing blood samples in case a blood transfusion becomes necessary [4].

The motivation behind this research stems from the need to address the limitations of traditional anemia detection methods such as the complete blood count (CBC), limitations identified in long waiting times, cumbersome paperwork, and inefficient communication with family doctors. By leveraging the versatility and reach of desktop applications and recently developed non-invasive anemia detection techniques, we aim to transform the way these services are delivered, ensuring the possibility of carrying out the anemia detection test autonomously, secure information exchange, and obtaining personalized care.

Reflecting the current healthcare focus (made achievable by innovative therapeutic care plans and services) on providing treatment to patients in the convenience of their own homes when possible [23], our primary objective is to develop an application that enhances and facilitates the information exchange between the doctor and the patients that test them self to detect anemia by leveraging the power of modern software engineering practices and technology. We aim to create a robust platform that facilitates effective communication between medical professionals and patients, ensures data privacy and security, and provides valuable insights through data analytics [6,24]. By achieving these objectives, we envision a more efficient and patient-centric healthcare system that optimizes resource allocation and improves health outcomes [9].

The development of a desktop application for medical services requires a systematic approach that incorporates both software engineering best practices and medical domain knowledge. We emphasize scalability, usability, and data protection. Collaborations with medical professionals and continuous feedback loops were integral to understanding the unique needs of the healthcare industry and ensuring the application meets and exceeds expectations.

This paper is organized into several sections subdivided as follows: the next section discusses the background and related work; Sect. 3 outlines our methodology and implementation details; following the UI of the application is described, then we present the results of structural and functional testing, and finally we conclude with a discussion of the potential impact of our application in the healthcare domain.

2 Related and Background Works

Creating a non-invasive system that enables patients to self-monitor their anemic status is becoming a hot topic in the last years [7]. Non-invasive anemia detection techniques can be subdivided into two macro-categories: (i) using pulse CO-Oximeters or similar devices to estimate the hemoglobin value thanks to light reflectance properties of the blood in the fingertip like in [14] or (ii) estimating the anemic status of the patient from digital images of various regions of interest (ROI) of the body. Some of the body region used to estimate the anemic status of a person are the finger [25] and the palm [21], but the most used ROI is the palpebral conjunctiva [12,15]. In the first macro category, we can find work like [17] where the authors using a specific arrangement of light emitting diodes and fiber optics, propose a multiwavelength spectrophotometry sensing platform to detect anemia that can estimate hemoglobin with a RMSE of 1.47 g/dL. Examples of systems belonging to the second macro category can be found in [18] where is proposed a smartphone application capable of estimating the hemoglobin value in the blood from photos of the fingernail bed with an accuracy of 2.4 g/dL^{-1} and in [10] the authors propose a system capable of estimate the anemic status of a patient by autonomously identify in pictures of the eye the sclera and its blood vessels and by investigating colour features coming from this two regions, showing an F1 score of about 80%.

All these systems focus only to the hemoglobin estimation or/and the anemia detection task; while allowing patients to be screened non-invasively at home (or in some other specific place), none of these devices allows the patient to directly show the obtained results to his/her doctor to have them live checked by an expert without moving. That is why we propose DeskEmo as a desktop application enabling doctors and lab physicians to remotely monitor patients' hematological parameters; by using IMAP as a communication protocol and by encrypting data with keys that periodically change we try to solve the scalability and data protection problems that usually afflict remote patient monitoring systems [13].

This project is based on Hbmeter [8], a software developed for iOS and Android that non-invasively estimates Hb levels by analyzing conjunctiva images. Hbmeter is designed to be used at home to estimate and track their Hb values. Along with Hbmeter, a spacer for the smartphone camera is proposed to help patients improve the eye picture quality, featuring LED lights, specialized macro lenses, and an eye-area rubber ring. The app has an initial image acquisition/selection phase; next, the user selects a conjunctiva area, which is refined via the SLIC superpixel generation algorithm [16] and third, a k-nearest neighbors algorithm predicts anemia risk as high (Hb < 10.5 g/dl), doubtful (10.5 < Hb < 11.5), or low (Hb > 11.5). During analysis, the app stores the acquired data to ensure they can be consulted at any time. Users can view image selections, analysis dates/times, and average a* channel values for each analysis. DeskEmo shows doctors these reports and images collected from Hbmeter.

3   DeskEmo Implementation

DeskEmo was born out of the need to be able to guarantee the monitoring of haematological parameters saved on the mobile application by the attending physician or a laboratory doctor. It is undeniable, however, that most of the software designed to simplify and speed up the work of a doctor ends up producing exactly the opposite effect due to its complexity of configuration, unintuitive interface, and incompatibility with the hardware and software in the doctor's office or laboratory. Therefore, DeskEmo makes simplicity its strength, it does not require any special installation procedure, it has a simple and clean graphical interface that recalls the style used for the app on mobile devices, and most importantly it is able to run on any desktop operating system including the most popular ones such as Windows, macOS, and Linux.

DeskEmo was created using Electron, an open-source framework that allows the building of desktop apps with web technologies like JavaScript, HTML, and CSS. Consequently, DeskEmo's user interface and capabilities are fully based on these technologies. A major advantage of utilizing web technologies for a desktop application is portability, consequently, DeskEmo can run smoothly across various common operating systems.

3.1 Data Transmission

The information received by DeskEmo from Hbmeter travels through secure channels that guarantee authentication, data integrity and encryption by operating on the standard protocol for Internet e-mail transmission [2]. The two most popular protocols for email communication are POP and IMAP. In the development of the application, it was decided to opt for the IMAP protocol because of the following motivations: (i) it allows access to mail both online and offline; (ii) allows several users to use the same mailbox at the same time; (iii) supports access to individual MIME parts of a message; (iv) allows subscribing to folders; (v) supports message attributes in the server and supports the definition of extensions.

This last functionality is very important because it allows the definition of extensions like IMAP Idle which lets the user receive a message from the server whenever there is an update in the mailbox without having to click on 'Send/Receive'. To ensure a secure channel during data exchange, the TLS protocol was adopted, which allows client/server applications to communicate over a network in a way that prevents data 'tampering', forgery, and interception. The TLS protocol allows bilateral authentication in which both parties securely authenticate themselves by exchanging certificates. This authentication (called Mutual authentication) requires that the client also possesses its own digital certificate.

3.2 Data Storage

DeskEmo does not make any use of structured databases. The motivation for this design choice can be attributed to one of the main objectives from the outset: to make DeskEmo a lightweight, portable application that is easy to install and configure. Indeed, the installation of a local database (e.g. MySQL) would require the intervention of an expert. Using an online database, in addition to requiring an expert during installation, would lead to DeskEmo's services having to depend on a server provider, this could lead to subsequent problems e.g. due to lack of maintenance, no connection, server overload, etc. Moreover, relying on a server provider would require a financial outlay because of the services offered.

For all these reasons, during the design of DeskEmo it was decided to organize the data using files that are saved and organized in special directories by the operating system, respectively:

- *"%APPDATA%"* on Windows;
- *"$XDG_CONFIG_HOME"* or *"/.config"* on Linux;
- *"/Library/Application Support"* on macOS.

These directories are rarely consulted by users of the operating system (by default are hidden by the operating system itself). The organization in special directories, hidden from the user, guarantees the integrity of the files and prevents any accidental modifications by the user. All sensitive data processed by DeskEmo are encrypted with a 256-bit Advanced Encryption Standard (AES) key and their transmission by Hbmeter (the mobile application) is via secure channels that guarantee the provenance and integrity of the data.

All sensitive information exchanged via email, once it arrives on the doctor's device, is stored locally for as long as it takes the doctor or specialist to check the patient's status and health, and then permanently deleted. This adds a further layer of security in ensuring the privacy of each individual patient. Historical data are in fact stored without reference to personal data, in order to guarantee privacy and security. The link with the original patient is maintained through the use of an encrypted key that is sent from time to time by the patient-side application (Hb Meter).

Figure 1 shows a simple visual summary of DeskEmo's architecture described in this section and how it allows doctors to monitor patients hematological parameters.

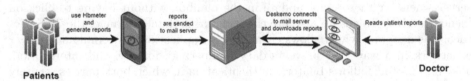

Fig. 1. DeskEmo architecture.

Moreover, new studies are being carried out to upgrade the anemia detection system, by making it personalized to the single patient by taking more than one eye picture in various subsequent days to than treat the data as time series. By collecting more than one eye picture, along with its relative Hb value, the same features currently used by Hbmeter can be represented as a time series, this data representation can allow to investigate, using recurrent neural network (RNN) and in particular Long short-term memory (LSTM) and echo-state networks (ESN), the possibility to predict the trend of hemoglobin and thus to assess, for example, how well a particular therapy is performing. The intrinsic characteristics of these models, combined with the new data representation, will allow to keep track of features derived from previous photos from the same patient and the corresponding hemoglobin value providing a way to memorize the specific characteristics of the patient eye, resulting in greater levels of accuracy in the prediction of the current hemoglobin value.

4   User Interaction with DeskEmo

We have chosen Bootstrap [22] as the front-end framework for DeskEmo web application. Bootstrap is a project started in 2010 by developers Mark Otto and Jacob Thornton. DeskEmo's interface is based on a responsive design and recalls the graphical style of Hbmeter to give a familiar feeling to the users. The need to adapt the page layout to different screen sizes and resolutions has introduced the concept of "Resolution breakpoints", in order to establish thresholds at which the graphical presentation can be modified according to the width of the device.

Responsive design is an important element of accessibility, which also takes into account numerous other factors, centered not only on devices but also on the characteristics of the user (such as cognitive abilities, eyesight, physical difficulties, and so on).

The DeskEmo interface is organized into two main sections for ease of use:

Report: This section displays all analysis patients have submitted to their doctor, organized in a data table allowing for efficient searching using one or more of the key fields in the header row (Fig. 2). The table layout enables doctors to quickly view essential information like the patient's name, email address, and analysis date. Each analysis is labeled to show if the doctor has already viewed it. By clicking the 'View' button, the doctor can access detailed information on the selected analysis, including the patient's personal data, average a* channel value calculated by Hbmeter, digital image taken by the patient, and conjunctival eyelid selection made on the captured image (Fig. 3).

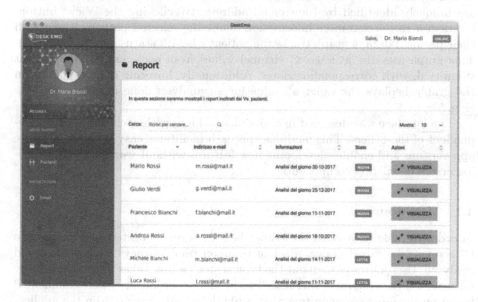

Fig. 2. Section showing the report list.

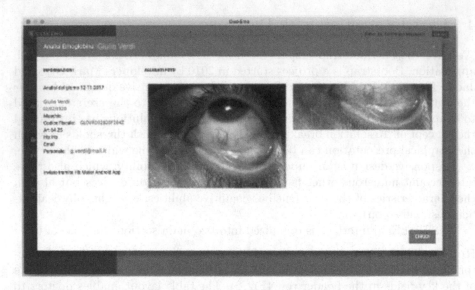

Fig. 3. Report of patients' analysis

Patients: This is the section dedicated to managing individual patients' personal data. Like the Report section, all information is organized in a data table. The table layout lets the doctor view various personal details of each patient, including their name, birth date, tax code, and email address (Fig. 4). Patients are uniquely identified by their email address. By clicking the 'View' button, the doctor can access more information about the selected patient. Along with their personal data, a graph tracks the patient's health status over time (Fig. 5). This graph uses the average a* channel values from each analysis the patient submitted, with corresponding dates. Additionally, hovering over any point on the graph displays the exact a* value for an analysis done on a specific date (Fig. 5).

The interface was designed in a modular fashion, with each component independent of the others. This modular approach facilitates easy updates in future app versions and enables developing new features without worrying about causing errors in existing components.

4.1   User Journeys

In order to make clearer to the reader how the user can interact with the two UI sections described above, a set of common user journeys were defined and analysed. User journeys map out the typical steps a user takes to accomplish key tasks within the system; in this case, Two primary user journeys were commented based on the most common task that a physician will carry out on the application: Checking newly received reports and visualising a patient report history. When the doctor wants to check if he/she has received new reports from his/her

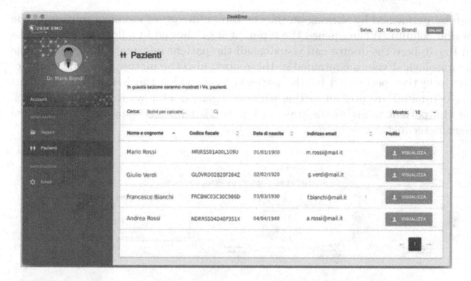

Fig. 4. Patients' personal data and health track record.

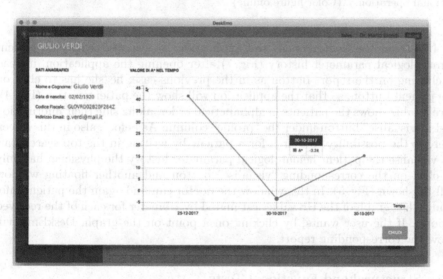

Fig. 5. Visualization of a patient's health condition over time.

patients (Fig. 6), after opening the application, the first thing that he/she has to do is to click on the report button in the left navigation menu, this will show the report section (Fig. 2); here the physician can see in the upper row of the table the newly received report, flagged by a green "new" status under the "status" column. From here the user can chose to search for a specific report by writing in the top search bar anything related to the report he/she wants to find (i.e. the patient name, its email, the report date...) or open a report; this operation can be performed by clicking on the corresponding grey "visualize" button in the action column. When opened the report will be showed in a floating window like in Fig. 3; here the doctor can visualize all the patient information along with the hematological values contained in the report; also the picture (and the conjunctiva selection performed by the patient) from which the hematological values are estimated are present in this window. If the doctor wants, he/she can click on the patient name in the top red bar to visualize the patient hematological parameter history.

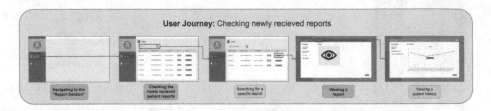

Fig. 6. First User Journey: Checking newly received reports (light blue boxes represent optional operations). (Color figure online)

If instead the doctor opens the application to visualise a specific patient hematological parameter history (Fig. 7) after opening the application, instead of clicking on the report button as in the previous case, he/she has to click on the patient button, so that the application will show the patient section (Fig. 4); here a table shows the patients in alphabetical order, along side their information and a "visualise" button under the "profile" column. As before, also in this screen there is the possibility to search for a patient by writing in the top search bar. To visualise the patient hematological parameter history the physician has only to click on the corresponding "visualise" button and another floating window will be shown (Fig. 5). In this window the doctor can find again the patient info, alongside a graph of the Hb values estimated by Hbmeter for each of the received reports. If the user wants, by clicking on a point on the graph, DeskEmo will show the corresponding report.

4.2   Structural and Functional Tests

Having ascertained the correct functioning of the Hbmeter, both White Box (structural test) and Black Box (functional test) tests were performed during the DeskEmo development phase. An incremental testing procedure was therefore adopted during the coding phase of DeskEmo. Each new function added in the code corresponded to a specific test in order to verify its correct functioning. For the correct functioning of the e-mail client, various e-mail providers were used (i.e., Gmail, Outlook and Libero) to ensure the correct functioning with them and thus fulfill DeskEmo's fundamental requirement: that of being a flexible software capable of adapting to many business contexts.

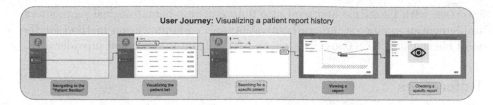

Fig. 7. Second User Journey: Visualizing the report history of a specific patient (light blue boxes represent optional operations). (Color figure online)

To perform functional tests, the development team of the patient-side application of Hbmeter was also involved in order to verify the proper functioning of communication with DeskEmo. The white box tests emulated a typical business scenario of a private practice where DeskEmo is started and left running on a normal computer. During the course of the day, various reports (from different mobile devices) were sent via Hbmeter to the email address configured on the DeskEmo software running on the private practice computer.

5 Conclusion and Future Work

Research on new techniques and devices for non-invasive anemia detection is currently thriving, but little of this research focuses on providing patients the ability to test at home while still being safely monitored by a physician. In this study, we propose DeskEmo as a complementary component to Hbmeter [8] to allow doctors and lab physicians to remotely monitor hematological parameters extracted from the mobile app on patients' smartphones. By combining the expertise in software engineering principles with the intricate demands of medical service delivery, our research offers a novel perspective on leveraging desktop applications to enhance non-invasive anemia detection systems. DeskEmo emphasizes simplicity since no complex installation is needed and has an intuitive interface mirroring the mobile app's design. In a doctor's office where time and efficiency are vital for diagnoses, DeskEmo excels by separating reports from regular email, tracking hematological parameter history, and organizing all data efficiently for easy, instant access. The immense potential of web technologies makes DeskEmo a flexible software that can continuously integrate new functions. At the time of writing a collaboration with the oncological hospital "Giovanni Paolo II" (in Bari, Italy) is being carried out involving both patients and doctors. This collaboration allows us to collect more samples to create a new dataset of conjunctival pictures, and thanks to doctors who agreed to use the proposed software we can collect new feedback from the users and perform a validation and assessment of the proposed tool.

Some potential future developments include creating a multi-account system to use multiple email addresses for receiving reports; integrating DeskEmo with the Personal Electronic Health Register [11]; building new mobile apps that can interface with DeskEmo and send also different, non-hematological parameters; implementing a more secure authentication and communication method for the mail client using REST architecture and APIs from major email providers [1].

References

1. Baldassarre, M.T., Barletta, V.S., Caivano, D., Piccinno, A.: Integrating security and privacy in HCD-scrum. In: CHItaly 2021: 14th Biannual Conference of the Italian SIGCHI Chapter, CHItaly 2021. Association for Computing Machinery, New York (2021). https://doi.org/10.1145/3464385.3464746
2. Baldassarre, M.T., Barletta, V.S., Caivano, D., Piccinno, A., Scalera, M.: Privacy knowledge base for supporting decision-making in software development. In: Ardito, C., et al. (eds.) INTERACT 2021. LNCS, vol. 13198, pp. 147–157. Springer, Cham (2022). https://doi.org/10.1007/978-3-030-98388-8_14
3. Barletta, V.S., Caivano, D., Colizzi, L., Dimauro, G., Piattini, M.: Clinical-chatbot AHP evaluation based on "quality in use" of ISO/IEC 25010. Int. J. Med. Inform. **170**, 104951 (2023). https://doi.org/10.1016/j.ijmedinf.2022.104951
4. Cook, J.D., Flowers, C.H., Skikne, B.S.: The quantitative assessment of body iron. Blood J. Am. Soc. Hematol. **101**(9), 3359–3363 (2003)
5. De Benoist, B., Cogswell, M., Egli, I., McLean, E.: Worldwide prevalence of anaemia 1993–2005; WHO global database of anaemia (2008)
6. Dimauro, G.: A new image quality metric based on human visual system. In: 2012 IEEE International Conference on Virtual Environments Human-Computer Interfaces and Measurement Systems (VECIMS) Proceedings, pp. 69–73. IEEE (2012)
7. Dimauro, G., Caivano, D., Di Pilato, P., Dipalma, A., Camporeale, M.G.: A systematic mapping study on research in anemia assessment with non-invasive devices. Appl. Sci. **10**(14), 4804 (2020)
8. Dimauro, G., Caivano, D., Girardi, F.: A new method and a non-invasive device to estimate anemia based on digital images of the conjunctiva. IEEE Access **6**, 46968–46975 (2018)
9. Dimauro, G., Caivano, D., Girardi, F., Ciccone, M.M.: The patient centered electronic multimedia health fascicle-EMHF. In: 2014 IEEE Workshop on Biometric Measurements and Systems for Security and Medical Applications (BIOMS) Proceedings, pp. 61–66. IEEE (2014)
10. Dimauro, G., Camporeale, M.G., Dipalma, A., Guarini, A., Maglietta, R.: Anaemia detection based on sclera and blood vessel colour estimation. Biomed. Signal Process. Control **81**, 104489 (2023)
11. Dimauro, G., Girardi, F., Caivano, D., Colizzi, L.: Personal health E-record—toward an enabling ambient assisted living technology for communication and information sharing between patients and care providers. In: Leone, A., Caroppo, A., Rescio, G., Diraco, G., Siciliano, P. (eds.) ForItAAL 2018. LNEE, vol. 544, pp. 487–499. Springer, Cham (2019). https://doi.org/10.1007/978-3-030-05921-7_39
12. Dimauro, G., Griseta, M.E., Camporeale, M.G., Clemente, F., Guarini, A., Maglietta, R.: An intelligent non-invasive system for automated diagnosis of anemia exploiting a novel dataset. Artif. Intell. Med. **136**, 102477 (2023)
13. El-Rashidy, N., El-Sappagh, S., Islam, S.R., El-Bakry, H.M., Abdelrazek, S.: Mobile health in remote patient monitoring for chronic diseases: principles, trends, and challenges. Diagnostics **11**(4), 607 (2021)

14. Hsu, D.P., French, A.J., Madson, S.L., Palmer, J.M., Gidvani-Diaz, V.: Evaluation of a noninvasive hemoglobin measurement device to screen for anemia in infancy. Matern. Child Health J. **20**, 827–832 (2016)

15. Jain, P., Bauskar, S., Gyanchandani, M.: Neural network based non-invasive method to detect anemia from images of eye conjunctiva. Int. J. Imaging Syst. Technol. **30**(1), 112–125 (2020)

16. Kim, K.S., Zhang, D., Kang, M.C., Ko, S.J.: Improved simple linear iterative clustering superpixels. In: 2013 IEEE International Symposium on Consumer Electronics (ISCE), pp. 259–260. IEEE (2013)

17. Kumar, R.D., et al.: A novel noninvasive hemoglobin sensing device for anemia screening. IEEE Sens. J. **21**(13), 15318–15329 (2021)

18. Mannino, R.G., et al.: Smartphone app for non-invasive detection of anemia using only patient-sourced photos. Nat. Commun. **9**(1), 4924 (2018)

19. Michie, S., Yardley, L., West, R., Patrick, K., Greaves, F.: Developing and evaluating digital interventions to promote behavior change in health and health care: recommendations resulting from an international workshop. J. Med. Internet Res. **19**(6), e232 (2017)

20. Payton, F.C., Pare, G., Le Rouge, C.M., Reddy, M.: Health care it: process, people, patients and interdisciplinary considerations. J. Assoc. Inf. Syst. **12**(2), 4 (2011)

21. Santra, B., Mukherjee, D.P., Chakrabarti, D.: A non-invasive approach for estimation of hemoglobin analyzing blood flow in palm. In: 2017 IEEE 14th International Symposium on Biomedical Imaging (ISBI 2017), pp. 1100–1103. IEEE (2017)

22. Thornton, J., Otto, M.: Bootstrap. https://getbootstrap.com/

23. Tortorella, G.L., Fogliatto, F.S., Mac Cawley Vergara, A., Vassolo, R., Sawhney, R.: Healthcare 4.0: trends, challenges and research directions. Prod. Plann. Control **31**(15), 1245–1260 (2020)

24. Vassakis, K., Petrakis, E., Kopanakis, I.: Big data analytics: applications, prospects and challenges. In: Skourletopoulos, G., Mastorakis, G., Mavromoustakis, C., Dobre, C., Pallis, E. (eds.) Mobile Big Data. Lecture Notes on Data Engineering and Communications Technologies, vol. 10, pp. 3–20. Springer, Cham (2018). https://doi.org/10.1007/978-3-319-67925-9_1

25. Wang, E.J., Li, W., Hawkins, D., Gernsheimer, T., Norby-Slycord, C., Patel, S.N.: HemaApp: noninvasive blood screening of hemoglobin using smartphone cameras. In: Proceedings of the 2016 ACM International Joint Conference on Pervasive and Ubiquitous Computing, pp. 593–604 (2016)

The Significance of Classical Simulations in the Adoption of Quantum Technologies for Software Development

Andrea D'Urbano[✉], Mario Angelelli, and Christian Catalano

University of Salento, Lecce, Italy
{andrea.durbano,mario.angelelli,christian.catalano}@unisalento.it

Abstract. This paper addresses classical simulations in the assessment of quantum computing performance. It emphasises the significance of these simulations in understanding quantum systems and exploring the potential of quantum algorithms. The challenges posed by the exponential growth of quantum states and the limitations of full-state simulations are addressed. Various approximation techniques and encoding methods are pointed out to enable simulations of larger quantum systems, and advanced simulation strategies tailored to specific goals are also discussed. This work focuses on the feasibility of classical simulation in decision processes regarding the development of software solutions, extending the assessment beyond high-performance computing systems to include standard hardware. This opportunity can foster the adoption of classical simulations of quantum algorithms to a wider range of users.

Keywords: Simulation · Quantum computing · Computational resources · Post-quantum cryptography · Software engineering

1 Introduction

The ongoing evolution of infrastructures, tools, and available resources for quantum computing (QC) is prompting the definition of innovation initiatives to foster the integration of classical and quantum processing systems and environments. Together with "pure" QC, the opportunity to *simulate* quantum computations on classical hardware can be relevant in many applications: first, it provides researchers and practitioners with empirical evidence on the expected output and the performance of quantum methods when compared to classical ones; furthermore, it can serve as a viable process towards hybrid QC [5]. The usefulness of simulated quantum computations, as well as their feasibility, is affected by various factors and, in particular, by the specific goals of the simulation. Indeed, depending on the complexity scaling of the specific problem being tackled, the information extracted from quantum simulations could be useless when compared to real quantum hardware (quantum processing units, or QPUs) for the inference of computational performance [11]. On the other hand, a quantum simulation carried out on a typical laptop can produce valuable insights

© The Author(s), under exclusive license to Springer Nature Switzerland AG 2024
R. Kadgien et al. (Eds.): PROFES 2023, LNCS 14484, pp. 60–67, 2024.
https://doi.org/10.1007/978-3-031-49269-3_6

when the aim is to characterise the noise and its effect on the measurement results of a quantum algorithm. Then, by emulating the behaviour of a quantum computer using classical hardware, researchers can compare the outcomes of quantum algorithms to classical solutions. This process allows for faster development of quantum algorithms and the identification of errors or inconsistencies, guaranteeing the accuracy of quantum algorithms before their deployment on real quantum hardware.

The present work aims to highlight the conditions and assumptions that can affect the effectiveness of main methods to simulate quantum computation on classical devices. Analysing these factors can support an appropriate evaluation of required resources, benefits, and limitations on information about quantum advantages inferred from simulations. In turn, this evaluation should become increasingly important in software development as a means to connect theoretical quantum algorithms with their real-world implementation. This objective is motivated by the need to properly assess and contextualise the results of simulated quantum computations to support decisions about the integration of classical computing with quantum subroutines also in the far-from-asymptotic regime where classical simulations can provide empirical evidence in real scenarios.

2   Methodology and Related Work

The emerging applications of QC require the acquisition of evidence to integrate algorithmic analysis with factors and conditions that affect the feasibility of the implementation of quantum routines on standard classical devices. This evidence can be obtained through a rapid review in the context of software engineering [6,14]. Based on the well-established phases of the review process, we first clarify the research question, namely: **RQ1**: *What are the main factors that affect the applicability of classical simulations to explore quantum advantage?*

Starting from the basic query on Web of Science for *"Classical simulation*"* AND *"quantum"*, 1,014 results were found; however, only 5 of them are included in the "Computer Science Software Engineering" category, while 106 are included in related fields ("CS Theory Methods", "CS Interdisciplinary Applications", "CS Information Systems", "CS Hardware Architecture", "CS Artificial Intelligence"). A qualitative selection of the abstracts and, subsequently, the assessment of the content of selected papers by a team of experts from the research laboratory in cybersecurity and secure software development pointed out the need for integration with other papers in line with the research question. These papers were found searching for specific problems (e.g., "elliptic cryptography") or methodologies (e.g., "tensor network*"). A brief outline of the results of this rapid review is presented in the following.

Zhang *et al.* provide an overview of the current techniques to benchmark random circuit sampling and classical simulations in relation to noisy quantum devices [34]. Several works address the need for appropriate data structures and representations to deal with classical simulations, from graph-based formulations based on the density matrix [32] to tensor networks and decision diagrams [12]. Kawaguchi *et al.* [23] demonstrate that a classical computer may effectively replicate a quantum version of Grover's method utilising the representation of tensor products in the density matrix renormalization group. Bartlett and Sanders [7] provide evidence about a large class of optical quantum physical phenomena (e.g., unitary transformations, amplification, noise, and measurements) that can be effectively emulated on a conventional computer. To allow the development of a novel computing device, in [8], the authors propose the definition and application of a quantum computer architecture. Castillo [15] gives a simulation of Grover's method highlighting its potential benefits for efficiently discovering a certain element in a crowded database and solving problems involving hard-to-find but easy-to-test solutions. The promise of quantum computers and algorithms for computational fluid dynamics applications, including the approximative quantum Fourier transform and a quantum algorithm for flow simulations, is discussed in [30]. Miranskyy *et al.* [27] examine the possible benefits and drawbacks of applying quantum algorithms to speed up software engineering jobs at various stages of the process. The authors propose a simulation environment enriched with parallel processing for modelling quantum adiabatic algorithms in [20], demonstrating how it can considerably increase the number of qubits that can be simulated using conventional hardware. Finally, a crucial use of classical simulations is in the demonstration of the emergence of quantum supremacy [4,35], as the simulated behaviour of a large-scale quantum system lets researchers illustrate the computational advantage of quantum computers over classical counterparts [9].

3   Classical Simulations in Performance Benchmark: Main Factors and a High-Level Process Representation

While classical computers are limited in their ability to simulate large-scale quantum systems efficiently, they can still be used to model smaller systems or specific aspects of quantum behaviour, such as noise modelling or the system response to external stimuli. These simulations can support a better understanding of quantum phenomena, guide the development of new quantum hardware and algorithms [10,24], and, more practically, serve as a benchmark to evaluate the performance of quantum hardware [33]. In this sense, classical simulations of quantum computation techniques have proven valuable as benchmarks for evaluating the performance of quantum computers and algorithms. In addition to their use in high-performance computing (HPC) systems, classical simulations can be effectively employed on "standard" hardware, making them accessible to a broader range of end users. Here we provide a high-level description of the integration of classical simulation within the software life-cycle, focusing on the identification of the main factors in the selection process of technologies (classical or quantum, HPC or standard) enabling a specific software solution under given resource constraints and assumptions. We focus on benchmarking in relation to applications of classical simulations, as it provides a basis for comparison and allows for the evaluation of the progress made in quantum computing technologies. Moreover, classical simulations enable the identification and characterisation of bottlenecks and limitations in quantum algorithms, facilitating their improvement and optimisation without the need for specialised quantum hardware.

We start specifying the methods to classically simulate a quantum computation. In this work, we concentrate on: *state vector*, where the simulation stores in memory the state vector describing the state of the system; *density matrix*, where the simulation keeps track of the evolution of the density matrix, another object used to describe a quantum system; *tensor network*, where the simulation makes use of a tensorial representation of a quantum circuit in order to find some clever way to reduce the computational cost; *stabilisers*, which can simulate only a subclass of quantum circuits, with very specific properties. Other simulation techniques can be envisaged to address different goals and computational models [2], but here we will discuss the four aforementioned ones since they are the most common and general-purpose ones.

The first node in the benchmark process is the specification of the problem: while this represents a fundamental basis in each software LCA, here the specification has a distinguished role due to the drastic change in the usefulness of the simulation depending on the domain in the space of parameters (e.g., number of qubits, circuit depth) and its effects on the noise and accuracy of the simulation. On the other hand, for the analysis in the design phase of the software development life cycle, approximate methods can be employed, as well as indicators such as specific representations of the expectation value, to get practical information about the final state without the need to keep track of the full quantum state.

The number of required qubits is the first discriminant factor in classical simulations: a state vector representation for a N-qubit quantum computation amounts to storing a vector of 2^N complex numbers encoded as a couple of floating point numbers in single or double precision. This state must be updated during the simulation, describing the application of the unitary operator to the state. A specific quantum gate can produce an efficient update, for example, by moving amplitudes or multiplying some entries by i or -1. However, this is not possible in general, and a full unitary operator applied to the state vector, corresponds to a matrix-vector multiplication, where the (unitary) matrix has dimensions $2^N \times 2^N$: it is clear that this approach can become quickly impractical, given the exponential scaling. The specification of the parameter domain of the problem given the assumptions and conditions on available resources supports the identification of appropriate characterisations to classify and select simulation protocols, e.g., distinguishing simulators that take into account noise, and those that are noiseless [21]. If noise needs to be considered, a more convenient simulation approach lies in the density matrix simulation, where a $2^N \times 2^N$ matrix with complex entries describes the quantum state as well as the noise.

As the size of the system increases, state vector and density matrix simulators face limitations due to the high memory requirements. However, by sacrificing accuracy, a larger system can be tackled. For example, noisy circuits can be simulated by employing the Monte Carlo method, which aggregates results from a sufficient number of pure-state simulator runs, to get a close approximation of the exact result [25]. Additionally, efforts have been made at the algorithmic level to improve full-state simulation, for example by using an adaptive encoding scheme [19] which reduces the memory needed to store a quantum state. However, this comes at the expense of increased run time required for the encoding and decoding steps. Another approach is the use of a low-rank decomposition method [18], which enables the simulation of noisy quantum circuits with density-matrix evolution, focusing on the most relevant columns. These cases lead to the inclusion of speed and memory required in the elicitation of assumptions underlying the tackled problem.

A different approach is represented by tensor networks [26], which is a representation of a quantum circuit with specified structure and qubit interactions that employs a graph of smaller-order tensors, thus reducing memory and computational demand. The flexibility of this representation enables different contraction strategies and provides techniques to control the approximation level, increasing efficiency but reducing accuracy. The tensor network can be simulated by contracting all the indices down to a scalar, usually an expectation value or an amplitude, or it can be left "open", simulating a full state. The open boundary condition, also referred to as full-amplitude simulation, has a space and time complexity that grows exponentially with the number of qubits, while the closed boundary condition, known as single-amplitude simulation, may require fewer resources [22]. An alternative is the "big-batch" boundary condition [28], which enables the computation of numerous correlated bit-string amplitudes. In certain circuits, the big-batch computation exhibits a contraction cost similar to single-amplitude simulation, allowing for the enumeration of all batches to obtain full amplitudes. The efficiency of the evaluation process in a tensor network depends on the order of tensor contraction, as different contraction sequences can result in varying levels of computational and storage requirements. Determining the optimal contraction order for a given network can be a complex task, but various heuristic approaches have been proposed for this purpose [29]. The efficient classical simulation of specific quantum circuits follows from the Gottesman-Knill theorem, which states that only quantum circuits composed by Clifford Gates can be simulated in polynomial time by a probabilistic classical computer [1], and leads to a distinction between weak and strong classical simulations [31]. Thus, these techniques highlight the role of the specification of circuit complexity, including their depth, and the error model.

The set of available methods and the associated advantages and constraints on simulations should be matched with available resources and the problem specification to select the simulation procedure and, hence, carry out the performance assessment. Multi-criteria decision-making approaches can be used to aggregate the performances and prioritise them, fostering in this way the comparison of the performance of classical simulations with quantum ones. In particular, some criteria such as scaling could be less relevant when a specific sub-problem has a well-defined dimensionality compatible with available methods (and, hence, lies in a far-from-asymptotic regime). Non-parametric methods (e.g., mid-quantile regression) and suitable accuracy indices [3] are robust approaches to prioritisation of rank or ordinal data, such as those derived from the comparative analysis. A graphical description of the aforementioned process is given in Fig. 1.

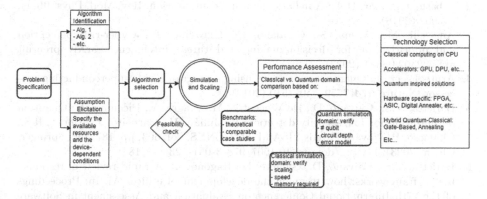

Fig. 1. High-level diagram of the inclusion of classical simulations and comparison with quantum simulations (if available) in technology selection

4   Conclusion

Through quantum software development and classical simulations, researchers can explore the capabilities and limitations of quantum systems, benchmark their performance, and verify the correctness of quantum algorithms, providing in this way a bridge between theoretical quantum algorithms and their practical implementation. The classical techniques developed in the current research can be directly translated into an intermediate layer in hybrid computation in the NISQ era [13]. The evaluation of required resources and regions of interest for the tackled problem in the parameter space plays a crucial role in assessing the outcomes of simulated quantum computations. This work intends to provide a basis for more detailed analyses of the feasibility and limitations of simulations run on generic classical devices, which will be the focus of future work with the aim of supporting informed decisions about the integration of classical computing with quantum systems.

A final remark involves the applicability of classical simulation to assess or compare alternative solutions to cybersecurity issues: indeed, the opportunities of interconnected digital systems and AI should be carefully addressed in relation to the sources of uncertainty they pose in terms of security [16,17]. The potential of quantum computing in this context, e.g. in IoT security detection [5], prompts further analyses on the benchmark process that guides software design to enhance the security of networks.

Acknowledgments. Andrea D'Urbano acknowledges the funding received by Deep Consulting s.r.l. within the Ph.D. program in Engineering of Complex Systems.

References

1. Aaronson, S., Gottesman, D.: Improved simulation of stabilizer circuits. Phys. Rev. A **70**(5), 052328 (2004)
2. Albash, T., Lidar, D.A.: Adiabatic quantum computation. Rev. Mod. Phys. **90**(1), 015002 (2018)
3. Angelelli, M., Arima, S., Catalano, C., Ciavolino, E.: Cyber-risk perception and prioritization for decision-making and threat intelligence. arXiv preprint arXiv:2302.08348 (2023)
4. Arute, F., et al.: Quantum supremacy using a programmable superconducting processor. Nature **574**(7779), 505–510 (2019)
5. Barletta, V.S., Caivano, D., De Vincentiis, M., Magrì, A., Piccinno, A.: Quantum optimization for IoT security detection. In: Julián, V., Carneiro, J., Alonso, R.S., Chamoso, P., Novais, P. (eds.) ISAmI 2022. LNNS, vol. 603, pp. 187–196. Springer, Cham (2023). https://doi.org/10.1007/978-3-031-22356-3_18
6. Barletta, V.S., Caivano, D., Gigante, D., Ragone, A.: A rapid review of responsible AI frameworks: how to guide the development of ethical AI. In: Proceedings of the 27th International Conference on Evaluation and Assessment in Software Engineering, EASE 2023, pp. 358–367. Association for Computing Machinery, New York (2023). https://doi.org/10.1145/3593434.3593478
7. Bartlett, S.D., Sanders, B.C.: Efficient classical simulation of optical quantum information circuits. Phys. Rev. Lett. **89**(20), 207903 (2002)
8. Bertels, K., et al.: Quantum computer architecture: towards full-stack quantum accelerators. 2020 Design, Automation & Test in Europe Conference & Exhibition (DATE), pp. 1–6 (2019)
9. Boixo, S., et al.: Characterizing quantum supremacy in near-term devices. Nat. Phys. **14**(6), 595–600 (2018)
10. Bourassa, J.E., et al.: Blueprint for a scalable photonic fault-tolerant quantum computer. Quantum **5**, 392 (2021)
11. Bravyi, S., Smith, G., Smolin, J.A.: Trading classical and quantum computational resources. Phys. Rev. X **6**(2), 021043 (2016)
12. Burgholzer, L., Ploier, A., Wille, R.: Simulation paths for quantum circuit simulation with decision diagrams what to learn from tensor networks, and what not. IEEE Trans. Comput. Aided Des. Integr. Circuits Syst. **42**(4), 1113–1122 (2022)
13. Callison, A., Chancellor, N.: Hybrid quantum-classical algorithms in the noisy intermediate-scale quantum era and beyond. Phys. Rev. A **106**(1), 010101 (2022)
14. Cartaxo, B., Pinto, G., Soares, S.: Rapid reviews in software engineering. In: Felderer, M., Travassos, G. (eds.) Contemporary Empirical Methods in Software Engineering, pp. 357–384. Springer, Cham (2020). https://doi.org/10.1007/978-3-030-32489-6_13
15. Castillo, J.E., Sierra, Y., Cubillos, N.L.: Classical simulation of Grovers quantum algorithm. Rev. Brasil. Ensino Fisica **42**, e20190115 (2020)
16. Catalano, C., Chezzi, A., Angelelli, M., Tommasi, F.: Deceiving AI-based malware detection through polymorphic attacks. Comput. Ind. **143**, 103751 (2022)
17. Catalano, C., Afrune, P., Angelelli, M., Maglio, G., Striani, F., Tommasi, F.: Security testing reuse enhancing active cyber defence in public administration. In: ITASEC, pp. 120–132 (2021)
18. Chen, Y.T., Farquhar, C., Parrish, R.M.: Low-rank density-matrix evolution for noisy quantum circuits. NPJ Quant. Inf. **7**(1), 61 (2021)

19. De Raedt, K., et al.: Massively parallel quantum computer simulator. Comput. Phys. Commun. **176**(2), 121–136 (2007)
20. Díaz-Pier, S., Venegas-Andraca, S.E.: Classical simulation of quantum adiabatic algorithms using mathematica on GPUs. Int. J. Unconv. Comput. **7**, 315–330 (2011)
21. Gao, X., Duan, L.: Efficient classical simulation of noisy quantum computation. arXiv preprint arXiv:1810.03176 (2018)
22. Gray, J., Kourtis, S.: Hyper-optimized tensor network contraction. Quantum **5**, 410 (2021)
23. Kadowaki, T., Nishimori, H.: Quantum annealing in the transverse ising model. Phys. Rev. E **58**(5), 5355 (1998)
24. Kyaw, T.H., et al.: Quantum computer-aided design: digital quantum simulation of quantum processors. Phys. Rev. Appl. **16**(4), 044042 (2021)
25. Li, G., Ding, Y., Xie, Y.: Eliminating redundant computation in noisy quantum computing simulation. In: 2020 57th ACM/IEEE Design Automation Conference (DAC), pp. 1–6. IEEE (2020)
26. Markov, I.L., Shi, Y.: Simulating quantum computation by contracting tensor networks. SIAM J. Comput. **38**(3), 963–981 (2008)
27. Miranskyy, A.V., Khan, M., Faye, J.P.L., Mendes, U.C.: Quantum computing for software engineering: prospects. In: Proceedings of the 1st International Workshop on Quantum Programming for Software Engineering (2022)
28. Pan, F., Zhang, P.: Simulation of quantum circuits using the big-batch tensor network method. Phys. Rev. Lett. **128**(3), 030501 (2022)
29. Schutski, R., Khakhulin, T., Oseledets, I., Kolmakov, D.: Simple heuristics for efficient parallel tensor contraction and quantum circuit simulation. Phys. Rev. A **102**(6), 062614 (2020)
30. Steijl, R.: Quantum algorithms for fluid simulations. Adv. Quant. Commun. Inf. (2019)
31. Van Den Nes, M.: Classical simulation of quantum computation, the Gottesman-Knill theorem, and slightly beyond. Quantum Inf. Comput. **10**(3), 258–271 (2010)
32. Viamontes, G.F., Markov, I.L., Hayes, J.P.: Graph-based simulation of quantum computation in the density matrix representation. In: Quantum Information and Computation II, vol. 5436, pp. 285–296. SPIE (2004)
33. Villalonga, B., et al.: A flexible high-performance simulator for verifying and benchmarking quantum circuits implemented on real hardware. NPJ Quant. Inf. **5**(1), 86 (2019)
34. Zhang, M., Wang, C., Han, Y.: Noisy random quantum circuit sampling and its classical simulation. Adv. Quant. Technol. 2300030 (2023)
35. Zhong, H.S., et al.: Quantum computational advantage using photons. Science **370**(6523), 1460–1463 (2020)

Enhancing Bug-Fixing Time Prediction with LSTM-Based Approach

Pasquale Ardimento[✉] [iD]

Department of Informatics, University of Bari Aldo Moro, Bari, Italy
pasquale.ardimento@uniba.it

Abstract. This work presents an approach based on Long short-term memory (LSTM) for estimating the bug-fixing time in the bug triage process. Existing bug-fixing time predictor approaches underutilize useful semantic information and long-term dependencies between activities in the bug-fixing sequence. Therefore, the proposed approach is a deep learning-based model that converts activities into vectors of real numbers based on their semantic meaning. It then uses LSTM to identify long-term dependencies between activities and classifies sequences as having either short fixing time or long fixing time. The evaluation on bug reports from the Eclipse project shows that this approach performs slightly better than the current best in the literature, boasting improved metrics such as accuracy, precision, f-score, and recall.

Keywords: bug-fixing time · prediction · LSTM · software maintenance · software repository mining · deep learning

1 Introduction

Mining Software Repositories is a research field that focuses on using data mining and machine learning techniques to analyze software repositories, particularly data maintained by Bug Tracking Systems (BTS). One crucial aspect of this area is predicting bug-fixing time, which can help software engineers allocate tasks more effectively. Bug-fixing time refers to the calendar time taken to resolve a bug. Previous studies have used various algorithms, such as naïve Bayes [1], Bayesian networks [12], k-nearest neighbor linear regression [2], SVM [12], Supervised Latent dirichlet Allocation [4], logistic regression [8], 0-R [6], 1-R [6] and hidden Markov model (HMM) [9]. These algorithms often rely on bug report fields like "Severity," "Reporter," "Comment," "Description," and "Summary." However, challenges arise due to changes in field values over time and missing temporal values.

This study introduces a deep learning-oriented method that utilizes the chronological order of actions executed in the bug-fixing process of bugs that have already been successfully fixed and verified. These temporal sequence activities contain meaningful terms representing activities with short and long-term dependencies. The proposed approach outperforms the HMM-based approach by utilizing a variable length of activities instead of fixed-length estimation.

© The Author(s), under exclusive license to Springer Nature Switzerland AG 2024
R. Kadgien et al. (Eds.): PROFES 2023, LNCS 14484, pp. 68–79, 2024.
https://doi.org/10.1007/978-3-031-49269-3_7

The main contributions of this work lie in introducing a deep learning-based approach that incorporates semantic information and short long-term dependencies from temporal sequences of activities, enhancing bug-fixing time prediction. Additionally, adopting variable-length sequences and cumulative data training further improves the approach's accuracy and efficiency. The proposed method demonstrates promising results when compared to the state-of-the-art HMM-based approach for predicting bug-fixing time.

To achieve these results, the research analyzes the temporal sequence activities related to previously fixed bug reports and uses them for training and testing the proposed models. By considering the HMM-based approach, which is a leading approach for predicting bug reports using temporal sequences, this research proposes a deep learning-based approach based on deep LSTM network and word embedding. This approach effectively captures long short term dependencies and semantic meaning between terms in a sequence of activities during the bug-fixing process. Furthermore, this research addresses the challenge of predicting bug-fixing time at the early stage of the bug lifecycle, where not all sequence activities are available. Instead of using all temporal sequence activities, the proposed approach utilizes a set of available activities to make predictions. This flexibility in handling variable-length sequences provides a significant advantage over fixed-length approaches, such as HMM-based methods. Experiments are conducted using Eclipse bug reports, and the proposed approach is compared with the state-of-the-art HMM-based approach.

Overall, this research contributes novel methods to predict bug-fixing time, leveraging deep learning techniques and addressing the limitations of existing approaches. The promising results demonstrate the potential of the proposed approach for enhancing bug-fixing time prediction in software development projects.

The rest of the paper is structured as follows. Section 2 presents the related work. The proposed method and empirical investigation conducted are given in Sect. 3 and Sect. 4. Section 5 evaluates the effectiveness of the proposed method in relation to the best results known in the literature. Finally, Sect. 6 concludes this work.

2   Related Work

Bug-fixing time prediction has been extensively studied in academic research. Various machine learning-based methods have been proposed to address this challenge. Anvik et al. developed a machine learning approach to reduce triaging time by categorizing reported bugs and identifying the developers who can resolve them. Kim analyzed the time required to fix bugs in different projects [13]. Panjer et al. used binary classification algorithms to predict bug fix-time. Giger et al. utilized a Decision Tree algorithm with bug report data to predict bug-fixing time [7]. Marks et al. employed the Random Forest technique for bug-fixing time prediction [14]. Zhang et al. proposed a Markov-based model to predict the number of bugs that will be fixed over time [18]. Ardimento used both BERT and DistilBERT for bug-fixing time prediction, achieving promising results [3,5].

The proposed approach addresses the limitations of existing approaches by using a deep LSTM with word-embedding techniques. It has been evaluated on Mozilla projects and showed significant improvements in accuracy and f-measure compared to base approaches. The model supports variable-length sequences, eliminating the need for activity prediction. Additionally, a cumulative version of the model, using data from multiple prior years for training and the current year for testing, outperformed the non-cumulative version.

Other related research includes bug report validity prediction, bug locating using deep learning-based methods, and link retrieval between bug reports and commits. The effectiveness of these approaches has been demonstrated in different projects, achieving high accuracy rates.

In conclusion, bug-fixing time prediction is an important aspect of software development, and several machine learning-based methods have been proposed to tackle this problem. The proposed model offers significant improvements in accuracy and supports variable-length sequences, enhancing bug-fixing time prediction. Other approaches in bug report validity prediction, bug locating, and link retrieval between bug reports and commits have also shown promising results, contributing to the efficiency of the software development process.

3   Proposed Method

The proposed method involves using a sequence of activities in the bug-fixing process as input to classify bugs into two classes: class 0 for bugs with a short fix time and class 1 for bugs with a long fix time. The approach is based on a deep LSTM network to extract long short term dependencies, and word embedding is used to capture semantic meaning between terms in the bug-fixing sequence. In this context, this section presents both the fundamentals of LSTM (Long Short-Term Memory) and a comprehensive overview of our proposed method. The following sub-sections delve into the basic concepts of LSTM and elaborate on the details of the proposed approach.

3.1   Deep LSTM Basics

Recurrent Neural Networks (RNNs), an extension of neural networks, process sequential data element by element, selectively passing information across sequence steps. However, they struggle with capturing long-term dependencies due to vanishing/exploding gradients during backpropagation. To address this issue, LSTM networks were proposed, which include memory cells to maintain states over time. LSTM cells have a detailed architecture where the previous output is combined with input values and fed into input, forget, and output gates, as well as the block input. The input gate controls new input into memory, while the forget gate determines what information to retain in the memory cell. LSTM networks overcome the limitations of traditional RNNs and have proven effective in various tasks.

Deep LSTMs can be constructed by stacking multiple LSTM layers vertically, where the output sequence of one layer becomes the input sequence of the next. This approach, with more parameters, outperforms single-layer LSTMs when there is enough data. Dropout is typically applied to non-recurrent edges, including between layers.

3.2 Word Embedding

Word embedding is a technique that represents words as vectors of numbers. Similar words have vectors close to each other, and word vectors provide word features. The two main word embedding techniques are continuous bag of words (CBOW) and skip-gram models. In skip-gram, the central word is the input, and context words are the output. In CBOW, it's the opposite, where context words are the input, and the central word is the output. Word order does not affect the results. The CBOW model merges the distributed representations of context, i.e., the words surrounding the target word, to make predictions about the word in the middle. On the other hand, the Skip-gram model takes the distributed representation of the input word itself and uses it to predict the context, or the surrounding words.

The bug report received from the ITS system contains crucial information regarding the software's usage and the bugs observed by users. Conversely, the commits made in the version control system provide insights into the software development process aimed at resolving the reported bugs. By establishing connections between bug reports and their corresponding commits, a valuable enhancement in knowledge pertaining to software development and application is achieved. However, it is worth noting that in many cases, the manual linkage between these instances and the explicit specification of bug IDs during software development for bug-fixing purposes is lacking.

To address this issue, Ruan et al. [15] proposed a deep learning-based approach designed to retrieve the linkages between bug reports and their corresponding commits. Their work presents a model that utilizes word embedding and deep LSTM to establish these connections effectively. The source code is transformed into a vector using word embedding, while the bug report text is also converted into a separate vector. These vectors are then utilized as inputs to a Deep LSTM network. The network is trained based on the established bug links between bugs and commits in previously fixed cases and is subsequently utilized to predict unspecified linkages. Notably, their approach exhibited an impressive improvement compared to the existing methods in terms of performance.

3.3 Proposed Deep LSTM-Based Method

The proposed method, utilizes a Deep LSTM with three stacked layers, designed for sequences of 500 states. Each state is mapped to a 128-length vector. The lower row of LSTM cells has hidden layers equal to the embedding vector length

(120 states), with 64 states as outcomes for right-handed and upon cells. The middle row has 64 hidden states with outcomes of 32 states for upon and right cells. The upon row has 32 hidden states, and its output to the right-hand and dense layer is a 4-unit length sequence. The dense layer classifies output as class 0 or 1 based on the sigmoid output. A dropout parameter of 0.5 enhances generality during training. The proposed method was implemented using Google Colab service.

3.4   Data Set

The proposed method is compared to the HMM-based method from [9]. To construct a dataset that captures the complete lifecycle of reported bugs, as opposed to merely offering snapshots of the most recent changes in bug report fields, the same approach as described in [17] was employed. The bug-fixing activities are sequenced over time, and in this research, the temporal sequence of activities is used, with each activity represented by a symbol. The symbols are defined and illustrated in the study. The comparison aims to evaluate the performance of the proposed method against the state-of-the-art HMM-based approach. It should be noted that only bug reports with a Status field set to VERIFIED and a Resolution field set to FIXED were taken into account. These specific bugs were considered relevant for training the classifier to predict fixing time of a newly bug report.

i. In [8], the influence of the bug reporter's reputation during bug-fixing was explored, revealing a robust correlation between the reporter's reputation, the bug opener, and the bug-fixing time. Based on this finding, three distinct symbols, namely N, M, and E, have been assigned to represent the 'Bug Reporter' categories, representing beginners, average reporters, and experienced reporters, respectively.

ii. The task allocation by the trigger can be carried out in two ways: either by assigning it to a specific developer (referred to as A) or by placing it in the Mailbox, allowing someone to volunteer for the task (referred to as B).

iii. Previous studies have also examined the impact of the CC field [16]. In the dataset mentioned, the symbol C is used to represent cases where one person is copied in the CC field, while the symbol D is used for cases where multiple people are copied.

iv. The influence of code reviews has been investigated in [11]. In this study, symbols S and V are employed to denote requesting a review from the usual Reviser and Super Reviser, respectively. On the other hand, symbols H and Y represent answering the corresponding review requests.

v. In [10], authors explored file and comment interaction effects. More comments sped up bug resolution, while attachments increased complexity, symbolized by F (file) and W (comment).

vi. In previous studies [10], it was observed that certain report fields undergo changes throughout the bug's lifecycle. These changing values were specifically examined for Milestone, Severity, and Priority, represented by symbols

L, P, and Q, respectively. Additionally, the Resolution status of the bug was denoted by the symbol Z.

The dataset contains bug reports with temporal sequences of activities, and each bug has a corresponding fixing time. Bugs with fixing times over third quartile days are labeled as class 1, while those fixed within third quartile days are labeled as class 0.

A bug report includes bug report identifier, fixing time class, and temporal activities during the bug-fixing process. For example, bug no. 433492 involves a beginner reporter, an initial description followed by 11 comments exchange between developers, and 4 persons are copied to the CC field (CC contains users who may not have a direct role to play on this bug, but who are interested in its progress).

4   Empirical Investigation

In this section, an empirical investigation is conducted to answer the following research question:

– Which sequence type, fixed-length or variable-length, yields better performance for the proposed model?

The proposed method aims to classify bug reports as slow or fast fixing based on their temporal sequences of activities. Two types of experiments were conducted to evaluate the algorithm's efficiency: one with fixed-length temporal sequences representing bug-fixing time on a specific day after reporting, and the other with sequences spanning a period (e.g., up to seven days) to measure prediction performance at that time. Data from prior years were used for training the model, either from a single prior year (non-cumulative model) or from five previous years (cumulative model).

In the dataset, only bug reports with status field set to VERIFIED and resolution field set to FIXED were considered. Efficient and early classification of bug reports is crucial for better planning and job scheduling, leading to the need for timely predictions based on limited temporal activity data.

The experiments were designed with two main parts. In the first part, fixed-length sequences of activities were used to predict bug-fixing time. Data from 2010 to 2016 were used, and the algorithm was trained on the entire sequence but tested using only the first few events of a bug's sequence to simulate early bug-fixing time prediction. Results shown in Table 1 proved that as more events were given to the algorithm during testing, the accuracy of predictions improved, indicating the benefit of considering long-term dependencies in the sequence, which is a characteristic of LSTM.

In the second part, variable-length sequences (the actual activities performed in the bug-fixing process until a specified date) were used for training and testing the proposed method.

The median days elapsed for the occurrence of 2, 3, and 4 activities are 2, 6, and 8 days, respectively. With more stringency, 1, 3, and 7 days are used as the activities of length 2, 3, and 4, respectively. Comparing the results of using a fixed-length sequence with a sequence with its corresponding variable-length shows much better results for using variable-length sequences. In the final model, a sequence of different lengths and activities up to the seventh day after getting the report will be used. This is like using four activities in the HMM-based model to guess how long it will take to fix a new bug.

By comparing the results of the two parts, it was concluded that using the actual activities (variable-length sequence) resulted in better performance than using fixed-length sequences. The difference in results between the proposed method and the HMM-based method (Habayeb's method) can be attributed to the heterogeneity of HMM and LSTM structures. HMM performed better with fixed-length sequences, while LSTM, with its support for variable-length sequences, yielded superior results.

Table 1 presented the results of the experiment, showing the accuracy of bug class predictions for different numbers of given events in the bug-fixing process. The results indicated that increasing the number of given events during testing led to improved accuracy, further confirming the LSTM's ability to capture long-term dependencies in the sequence of activities.

Overall, the experiments demonstrated that considering actual activities over a variable length of time in the bug-fixing process improved the accuracy of bug-fixing time predictions, highlighting the effectiveness of LSTM in capturing long-term dependencies in sequential data.

Table 1. Fixed-length sequence VS variable-length sequence.

Type	f1 score	accuracy	precision	recall
2 event	0	0.64	0	0
day 0	0.67	0.72	0.58	0.81
3 event	0.28	0.69	0.82	0.1
day 3	0.77	0.81	0.71	0.815
4 event	0.58	0.77	0.79	0.47
day 7	0.83	0.86	0.74	0.95
5 event	0.66	0.78	0.75	0.5
6 event	0.66	0.79	0.77	0.58

In summary, this part of the experiments demonstrated the advantage of using actual activities performed during specific time intervals after receiving bug reports instead of using fixed-length estimations. The approach allowed for more accurate bug class predictions in the early phases of the bug's life cycle, aiding in better bug-fixing planning.

5   Performance Evaluation

In this section, the effectiveness of proposed method is assessed by comparing it with the state-of-the-art approach introduced by Habayeb et al. [9] and Sepah-vand et al. [17], which are currently considered the best methods for predicting bug-fixing time. These approaches utilizes temporal activities in the bug-fixing process to predict bug-fixing time and has demonstrated superior performance compared to previous methods. In this analysis, the results of proposed method with both the two models are compared.

The comparison is divided into two parts. In the first part, the performance of both methods by predicting bug-fixing time for bug reports received in one year based on data from previous years has been evaluated. The main objective is to predict the bug-fixing time by observing the temporal activities performed during the bug-fixing process.

The second part of the analysis focuses on examining the impact of the timing of bug-fixing time prediction after receiving a bug report. Shorter forecasts can lead to better resource planning, while longer waiting times may result in more accurate predictions. Finding a balance between the prediction time and the model's accuracy is essential.

In the following sections, these comparisons are explored further and the results obtained from both evaluations are discussed.

5.1   Comparison of Two Methods for Predicting Bug-Fixing Time Using Data from Previous Years

In the real-world scenario, data from previous years are present, including the time taken to fix bugs, and the aim is to predict the time required to fix new bugs based on this historical data. A variable-length sequence is used and activities up to the 7th day after receiving the bug report are considered (equivalent to using 4 activities in the HMM-based model) for predicting the bug-fixing time of new reports.

In Table 2, the average results for both the base methods and the proposed method are shown. Notably, the proposed method exhibits significant improvements in performance, with an average increase of 17.11 in accuracy, 27.27 in F-score, 10.16 in precision, and 18.64 in recall. These results reinforce the superiority of our approach over the HHM method.

Furthermore, it is worth mentioning that when compared to the LSTM model proposed by Sepahvand et al. [17], although the improvement is still substantial, it appears relatively modest. In this particular scenario, the outcomes can be considered nearly equivalent, underscoring the effectiveness of both approaches within this specific context.

Table 2. Comparing the average performance of proposed model with HMM-based model and LSTM model in predicting fixing bug of one year based on prior years data.

	f1 score	accuracy	precision	recall
HHM	70	70.62	69.62	69.37
DEEPLSTM [17]	96.37	87.25	79.75	87.25
proposed model	97.27	87.81	79.78	87.99

5.2 Impact of the Duration Between Bug Report Receipt and Prediction on Model Effectiveness

In this section, a comparative analysis of the two proposed methods and the base algorithms is conducted, where both models utilize variable-length sequences. Specifically, temporal activities performed in the bug-fixing process until the first, third, and seventh days after receiving the bug report for testing are used. The timeliness of predictions plays a crucial role in effective task planning. As depicted in Table 3, the results of testing the two algorithms with the mentioned data demonstrate that the proposed LSTM model consistently outperforms the HMM-based method in all cases. Moreover, the efficiency of the proposed approach improves with the increasing number of days used for testing. When prediction of bug-fixing time is based on activities performed on day 0 of receiving the bug report, the proposed approach closely resembles the HMM method. However, as the prediction is extended to activities performed on the second day after receiving the report, the proposed method exhibits an 11% improvement in efficiency over the HMM method. Notably, the performance gap widens further, reaching a 16% improvement, when predictions are based on activities performed up to the seventh day after receiving the bug report. Furthermore, proposed model, when compared to the LSTM model introduced by Sepahvand et al. [17], exhibits a slight advantage in performance.

Table 3. Comparing the result of methods by testing the models with temporal activities done in bug-fixing process until 1, 3 and 7 days after receiving a bug report

Algorithm	Train	f1 score	accuracy	precision	recall
DEEPLSTM [17]	day 0	0.67	0.72	0.58	0.81
proposed model [17]	day 0	0.68	0.73	0.60	0.82
HMM	day 0	0.66	0.61	0.76	0.58
DEEPLSTM [17]	day 3	0.77	0.81	0.71	0.81
proposed model [17]	day 3	0.79	0.82	0.72	0.83
HMM	day 3	0.68	0.62	0.81	0.58
DEEPLSTM [17]	day 7	0.83	0.86	0.74	0.95
proposed model [17]	day 7	0.85	0.88	0.77	0.96
HMM	day 7	0.67	0.61	0.81	0.58

5.3   Study Limitations

Analyzing the limitations of the proposed method compared to previous approaches, certain drawbacks inherent in temporal activity-based models may be observed, including both the HMM and our proposed method. Extracting bug-fixing activities after receiving a report is a time-consuming process, which can impact the efficiency of these methods. Additionally, the proposed approach requires a substantial amount of training data, making it less effective when training data is limited, as demonstrated in the non-cumulative rows of Table 1.

To address the issue of missing data, the cumulative model was adopted, utilizing all available data from previous years for training, improving the method's performance. However, for projects with a scarcity of issues, the proposed approach may not yield satisfactory results. Another challenge lies in the resource-intensive nature of deep learning algorithms, demanding significant processing resources and lengthy training times.

6   Conclusion

The proposed approach addresses the limitations of existing bug-fixing time prediction methods by incorporating deep learning techniques. It uses a deep LSTM model along with word-embedding techniques to capture semantic information and short long-term dependencies in the sequence of bug-fixing activities. The evaluation, conducted on bug reports from Eclipse projects, reveals some impressive results. Compared to the HMM model approach, there's a significant 15–20% boost in accuracy and f-measure. Even when measured against the best-known LSTM approach in the literature, this new model shows a slight improvement. It seems like a robust and competitive strategy to enhance bug-fixing time predictions. One of its strengths is its ability to handle variable-length sequences, eliminating the need for activity estimation. Additionally, the cumulative version of the proposed method, which uses data from multiple previous years for training and the current year for testing, outperformed the non-cumulative version. Overall, the proposed method offers better bug-fixing time prediction and has the potential to significantly improve software development processes.

In the future, the approach could be further enhanced by considering the analysis of different types of users' requests submitted via BTS. This could involve categorizing requests into various types, such as fixing, enhancement, documentation, and organizational requests. By incorporating this additional information, the predictive capabilities of the system may be improved, leading to more accurate and context-specific outcomes.

Moreover, an interesting avenue of exploration could involve examining bug reports to address potential issues with unbalanced datasets. Assessing the necessity of improving prediction performance by addressing the challenges posed by imbalanced bug report data would be a valuable undertaking.

References

1. Abdelmoez, W., Kholief, M., Elsalmy, F.M.: Bug fix-time prediction model using Naïve Bayes classifier. In: 22nd International Conference on Computer Theory and Applications (ICCTA), pp. 167–172 (2012). https://doi.org/10.1109/ICCTA.2012. 6523564
2. Anbalagan, P., Vouk, M.A.: On predicting the time taken to correct bug reports in open source projects. In: 25th IEEE International Conference on Software Maintenance, 20–26 September 2009, Edmonton, Alberta, Canada, pp. 523–526. IEEE Computer Society (2009). https://doi.org/10.1109/ICSM.2009.5306337
3. Ardimento, P.: Predicting bug-fixing time: Distilbert versus google BERT. In: Taibi, D., Kuhrmann, M., Mikkonen, T., Klünder, J., Abrahamsson, P. (eds.) PROFES 2022. LNCS, vol. 13709, pp. 610–620. Springer, Cham (2022). https://doi.org/ 10.1007/978-3-031-21388-5_46
4. Ardimento, P., Boffoli, N.: Predicting bug-fixing time using the latent Dirichlet allocation model with covariates. In: Kaindl, H., Mannion, M., Maciaszek, L.A. (eds.) ENASE 2022. CCIS, vol. 1829, pp. 139–152. Springer, Cham (2022). https:// doi.org/10.1007/978-3-031-36597-3_7
5. Ardimento, P., Mele, C.: Using BERT to predict bug-fixing time. In: 2020 IEEE Conference on Evolving and Adaptive Intelligent Systems. EAIS 2020, Bari, Italy, 27–29 May 2020, pp. 1–7. IEEE (2020). https://doi.org/10.1109/EAIS48028.2020. 9122781
6. Bougie, G., Treude, C., Germán, D.M., Storey, M.D.: A comparative exploration of freeBSD bug lifetimes. In: Proceedings of the 7th International Working Conference on Mining Software Repositories, MSR 2010 (Co-located with ICSE), Cape Town, South Africa, 2–3 May 2010, Proceedings, pp. 106–109. IEEE Computer Society (2010). https://doi.org/10.1109/MSR.2010.5463291
7. Giger, E., Pinzger, M., Gall, H.C.: Predicting the fix time of bugs. In: Proceedings of the 2nd International Workshop on Recommendation Systems for Software Engineering. RSSE 2010, Cape Town, South Africa, 4 May 2010, pp. 52–56. ACM (2010). https://doi.org/10.1145/1808920.1808933
8. Guo, P.J., Zimmermann, T., Nagappan, N., Murphy, B.: Characterizing and predicting which bugs get fixed: an empirical study of Microsoft windows. In: Proceedings of the 32nd ACM/IEEE International Conference on Software Engineering - Volume 1, ICSE 2010, Cape Town, South Africa, 1–8 May 2010, pp. 495–504. ACM (2010). https://doi.org/10.1145/1806799.1806871
9. Habayeb, M., Murtaza, S.S., Miranskyy, A.V., Bener, A.B.: On the use of hidden Markov model to predict the time to fix bugs. IEEE Trans. Softw. Eng. 44(12), 1224–1244 (2018). https://doi.org/10.1109/TSE.2017.2757480
10. Hooimeijer, P., Weimer, W.: Modeling bug report quality. In: 22nd IEEE/ACM International Conference on Automated Software Engineering (ASE 2007), 5–9 November 2007, Atlanta, Georgia, USA, pp. 34–43. ACM (2007). https://doi.org/ 10.1145/1321631.1321639
11. Jeong, G., Kim, S., Zimmermann, T.: Improving bug triage with bug tossing graphs. In: Proceedings of the 7th joint meeting of the European Software Engineering Conference and the ACM SIGSOFT International Symposium on Foundations of Software Engineering, 2009, Amsterdam, The Netherlands, 24–28 August 2009, pp. 111–120. ACM (2009). https://doi.org/10.1145/1595696.1595715
12. Jonsson, L., Borg, M., Broman, D., Sandahl, K., Eldh, S., Runeson, P.: Automated bug assignment: ensemble-based machine learning in large scale industrial contexts.

Empir. Softw. Eng. **21**(4), 1533–1578 (2016). https://doi.org/10.1007/s10664-015-9401-9

13. Kim, S., Whitehead, E.J.: How long did it take to fix bugs? In: Proceedings of the 2006 International Workshop on Mining Software Repositories. MSR '06, pp. 173–174. Association for Computing Machinery, New York, NY, USA (2006). https://doi.org/10.1145/1137983.1138027

14. Marks, L., Zou, Y., Hassan, A.E.: Studying the fix-time for bugs in large open source projects. In: Proceedings of the 7th International Conference on Predictive Models in Software Engineering. PROMISE 2011, Banff, Alberta, Canada, 20–21 September 2011, p. 11. ACM (2011). https://doi.org/10.1145/2020390.2020401

15. Ruan, H., Chen, B., Peng, X., Zhao, W.: Deeplink: recovering issue-commit links based on deep learning. J. Syst. Softw. **158** (2019). https://doi.org/10.1016/j.jss.2019.110406

16. Scholtes, I., Zanetti, M.S., Tessone, C.J., Schweitzer, F.: Categorizing bugs with social networks: a case study on four open source software communities. In: Software Engineering 2014, Fachtagung des GI-Fachbereichs Softwaretechnik, 25. Februar - 28. Februar 2014, Kiel, Germany. LNI, vol. P-227, pp. 27–28. GI (2014). https://dl.gi.de/handle/20.500.12116/30980

17. Sepahvand, R., Akbari, R., Hashemi, S.: Predicting the bug fixing time using word embedding and deep long short term memories. IET Softw. **14**(3), 203–212 (2020). https://doi.org/10.1049/iet-sen.2019.0260

18. Zhang, H., Gong, L., Versteeg, S.: Predicting bug-fixing time: an empirical study of commercial software projects. In: 35th International Conference on Software Engineering. ICSE '13, San Francisco, CA, USA, 18–26 May 2013, pp. 1042–1051. IEEE Computer Society (2013). https://doi.org/10.1109/ICSE.2013.6606654

Enhancing Code Obfuscation Techniques: Exploring the Impact of Artificial Intelligence on Malware Detection

Christian Catalano[1], Giorgia Specchia[2]($\boxtimes$), and Nicolò G. Totaro[2]($\boxtimes$)

[1] Department of Innovation Engineering, University of Salento, Lecce, Italy
[2] Centre for Applied Mathematics and Physics for Industry (CAMPI),
University of Salento, Lecce, Italy
{giorgia.specchia,nicologiamauro.totara}@unisalento.it

Abstract. Code obfuscation techniques serve to obscure proprietary code, and there are several types. Various tools, such as reverse engineering, are used to reconstruct obfuscated code. To make the analysis and decoding of obfuscated code more difficult, obfuscation techniques can be combined in cascades. Artificial Intelligence (AI) can be used to recombine old codes with each other and make it more difficult to decrypt them. In this paper, the focus is precisely on the increased complexity of the process of reconstructing proprietary code if it is generated with the aid of AI, and consequently on the increasing difficulty for antiviruses in detecting this new type of malware.

Keywords: Metamorphic Generator · Malware Obfuscation · Malware Detection · Artificial Intelligence · Cybersecurity

1 Introduction

In recent years, a concept that is attracting increasing attention in the academic and industry communities is that of the *Sharing Economy*. Sharing Economy means "a socio-economic system enabling an intermediated set of exchanges of goods and services between individuals and organizations which aim to increase efficiency and optimization of sub-utilized resources in society" [3,12], for example in works like [5], the sharing of resources can be exploited to reach new assets for both public and private organizations. The high failure rate of Big Data and AI projects is a problem organisations are facing [11]. For this reason, various maturity models have been developed to analyse the technological maturity of companies, such as, for example, in [8]. One of the possible solutions has been identified in the principles of the sharing economy, in particular through the sharing of data, technologies, and intelligent agents between different organisations [10]. Sharing weakens the protection of resources, as happened in the field of software engineering for the protection of intellectual property [4]. To counteract this, several techniques have been developed, including that of **obfuscation**, which is inevitably linked to the field of *Malware Detection* [19]. Obfuscation refers to the act of making the source code or machine code of software difficult to decipher and interpret. Obfuscation techniques are divided into

R. Kadgien et al. (Eds.): PROFES 2023, LNCS 14484, pp. 80–88, 2024.
https://doi.org/10.1007/978-3-031-49269-3_8

static and dynamic techniques. The former modifies the source code or binary of a program without changing its behaviour, e.g. cybercriminals use these techniques to prevent antivirus software from easily analysing and detecting their code, thus trying to bypass the signature-based detection techniques common to all recent antivirus software. The latter changes the behaviour of the software while it is running, which makes detection more complex. As already mentioned, this technique is also used in Malware Detection. Malware can be distinguished into various types. **Polymorphic malware** constantly changes its identifying characteristics to avoid detection. The main body of the code (payload) appears meaningless, and its functionality is restored through decryption [6]. It can create an infinite number of distinct decryptors with the help of obfuscation techniques, such as dead code insertion or register reassignment [18]. **Oligomorphic malware**, also known as *semi-polymorphic malware*, is similar to the previous one but less sophisticated. This type of malware can generate at most a few hundred different decryptors. Finally, **metamorphic malware** does not have an encrypted part, so it does not need a decryptor. Instead of only changing the decryptor loop, metamorphic malware mutates its entire body. Each new copy may have a different structure, a different code sequence, a different size and different syntactic properties, but the malware's behaviour does not change [15].

In this context, obfuscation techniques are used to limit the **Cyber Attribution**. Cyber Attribution is the process of tracing, identifying and attributing authorship to the perpetrator of a cyber-attack [14]. This becomes important because new types of malware attacks represent constantly and rapidly evolving threats and the lack of in-depth and automated analysis makes it difficult to identify and trace back to the source of these attacks as well as to prevent them. Although efforts are already being made to raise awareness of cyber threats at school level (e.g. in [9] it has been proposed to change the typical lectures to a CTF-based training method) or extensions are being developed, as in [16], to enable the detection of particular types of threats to less experienced users.

Currently, most rely on manually conducted analysis techniques, which are extremely time-consuming and not scalable due to the large amount of malware in circulation. Automated systems, on the other hand, use heuristic techniques to detect malware, such as signature detection. However, these fail to detect the most innovative attacks because they provide no way to link new malware to known malware and no basis to characterise its authorship or predict its future development. In fact, since cybercriminals often reuse code and techniques used in previous attacks to speed up the creation of new innovative malware, recognising such elements makes it possible to develop defences more quickly and make assumptions about malware authorship.

2   State of the Art

There are different types of code obfuscation techniques. They are divided into high-level and low-level techniques. The former are applied directly to the source code of the program to be obfuscated. While the latter are applied directly on the machine code of the program, i.e. after a high-level code has been compiled, or on a shellcode. Furthermore, they can be cascaded so that each additional technique makes the analysis and decoding of the obfuscated code even more complex. The main high-level techniques are the following: **Renaming**, which is to replace the names of variables, functions and classes, and their corresponding implementation, with names that are less comprehensible to the reader [17]. Two examples of application are *static renaming* and *dynamic renaming*; **Control Flow**, which refers to the use of fictitious code and the insertion of unnecessary conditional instructions to complicate the understanding of how the code works, attempting to create multiple "dead-end" branches of the code flow, which can confuse both the reader and the decompilation tools used to trace the source code [17]; **Removing Unused and Debug Code**, Logs provide the path that a program is following to perform various actions. When trying to recreate what a program does by reverse engineering, the information from these logs can be extremely useful. In fact, by making a small change to the code, one can check the impact of the error by checking these debug logs. Therefore, the removal of debug files and tools may be particularly important for obfuscating source code. [17]; **String Encryption**, the idea is to encrypt and decrypt the strings in the program, because they could act as reference points in the code [17]. The main high-level techniques are the following. **Renaming**, the main action of this technique is to replace the names of variables, functions and classes, and their corresponding implementation, with names that are less comprehensible to the reader [17]. Two examples of application are *static renaming*, which replaces each word found in the code (that is not a keyword) with a random string, and *dynamic renaming*, which for each function or variable found in the code assigns a new name and changes iterations. **Control Flow**, it refers to the use of fictitious code and the insertion of unnecessary conditional instructions to complicate the understanding of how the code works, attempting to create multiple "dead-end" branches of the code flow, which can confuse both the reader and the decompilation tools used to trace the source code [17]; **Removing Unused and Debug Code**, Logs provide the path that a program is following to perform various actions. When trying to recreate what a program does by reverse engineering, the information from these logs can be extremely useful. In fact, by making a small change to the code, one can check the impact of the error by checking these debug logs. Therefore, the removal of debug files and tools may be particularly important for obfuscating source code. [17]; **String Encryption**, the idea is to encrypt and decrypt the strings in the program, because they could act as reference points in the code [17].

While the main low-level techniques are the following. **Fake Code Injection**, unnecessary instructions are added to a program to change its appearance, but maintain its behaviour. This technique can be easily circumvented, however, by signature-based analysis tools by eliminating unnecessary instructions beforehand. **Reassignment of Registers**, registers are elements of a processor's internal memory where data relevant to the running program is stored; this technique involves changing registers from generation to generation, while keeping the program code and its behaviour unchanged [19]; **Rearranging Subroutines**, subroutines are independent blocks of code that execute a specific sequence of instructions and can be called from any part of the main program. This technique obfuscates a code by changing the order of its subroutines randomly [18]; **Replacing Instructions**, obfuscation occurs by replacing certain instructions with others equivalent to them, e.g. the instruction "xor" can be replaced with "sub" [13]; **Code Transposition**, the main purpose of this technique is to change the order of the [7] code, which can be done in two ways: by randomly shuffling instructions and then recovering the original execution order by inserting unconditional branches or jumps, or by creating new generations, choosing and reordering independent instructions that have no impact on each other. Since it is a complex problem to find the independent instructions, the latter method may increase the cost and time of obfuscation detection to a greater extent than the former. **Integration of the Code**, you insert the malware code into another code of a "target" program [13].

3   Proposal

This paper aims to investigate and analyse the integration of AI in code obfuscation strategies, to increase the effectiveness of cybersecurity systems. In particular, the focus was on improving obfuscation techniques in order to make the process of reconstructing proprietary code more complicated. To test the effectiveness of obfuscation, a malware was generated with the help of AI. This not only emphasises the support offered by this technology but also highlights the need to modernise current antivirus software so that it can detect these new types of malware, created using this technology for offensive rather than defensive purposes. In fact, thanks to the constant increase in the accessibility and user-friendliness of AI, it is now possible to generate large amounts of source code quickly and efficiently. These features make it possible to quickly create new generations of malware from malicious code.

In this section, the implementation of a possible obfuscation system for the generation of source code by AI and its subsequent integration with sample malicious code is presented. To achieve this, Python was chosen as the programming language and GPT as the AI, specifically the *text-davinci-003* model. Due to the stochastic behaviour of the scripts generated by the AI, it was necessary to add a control phase to the system to ascertain whether the generated scripts actually proved valid for proper functioning. In the following paragraphs, the creation of the malicious code will be explained step by step. The first step is the generation of fake code, namely the part of the code that will then be integrated into the malicious code without affecting its behaviour. To do this, a generator script was developed. This script makes use of the API Key provided by the official OpenAI website to access GPT's AI API calls. As mentioned above, the AI model used is *code-davinci-003*, a template used to create Python scripts that follow instructions given by a prompt recited in natural language. The prompt used for this template is as follows: 1) create some random imports to use in the script, from 1 to 15, then create lists and variables and fill them with random data. Start this section with the comment: (# start); 2) define functions that use these variables and import, from 1 to 15. Start this section with the comment: (# end of imports); 3) add a comment: (# anywhere); 4) call these functions with random values and use some loops. Start this section with the com. T(# bottom). The context of the script is *! CONTEXT !*. In this implementation, the last part of the script has not been specified, the one concerning the context, but it is possible to have the AI generate fake scripts concerning any topic (e.g. IOT, back-end, server, etc.). This feature makes it possible to hide the actual function of the script from careless analysis. Figure 1 shows the code used for generating the fake code.

```
1    #library required to use the GPT API
2    import openai
3    import os
4    #the OpenAI GPT API personal key
5    openai . api_key = "..."
6    number_of_ai_generated_scripts = 61 # number of scripts to be generated and checked +1
7    #The function get_gpt_response () accepts a prompt as input and sends a request to the GPT API to obtain a response
8    #from Artificial Intelligence . Once received, the function returns the response generated by the AI.
9    def get_gpt_response ( prompt_mine ):
10   response = openai . Completion . create (
11   # name of the model to be used
12   model ="text - davinci -003 ",
13   prompt = prompt_mine ,
14   # value between 0 and 2, it slightly changes the response of the model, the higher it is, the more random and less
15   #deterministic the response
16   temperature =0.7 ,
17   # maximum number of characters the A.I. may write as an answer
18   max_tokens =3000 ,
19   )
20   message = response . choices [0]. text . strip ()
21   return message
22
23   for i in range (1, number_of_ai_generated_scripts ):
24   # check if the file 'number'.py already exists ', otherwise call the function get_gpt_response () and create the new file
25   if not os. path . exists ( str(i)+'.py '):
26   prompt = '' # The prompt to generate scripts
27   response = get_gpt_response ( prompt )
28   with open (''+str(i)+'.py ', 'w') as f:
29   print (" Writing AI generated python script : "+ str(i)+".py ...\ n")
30   f. write ( response )
31   f. write ('\n')
```

Fig. 1. Code used to generate the fake code

After generating a satisfactory number of fake scripts, another *controller* script was created to check their validity and correct functioning. In the event that some scripts are invalid, the controller deletes them and starts the fake script generator again, and then checks the validity of the newly produced scripts. This cycle of checking and renewing is repeated until a satisfactory number of valid fake scripts is reached. For the creation of the malicious code, a simple keylogger, which records the keys pressed by the user on the keyboard and sends them to a discord server with the help of a bot. The malicious code was then prepared for the assembler by adding specific comments to allow the insertion of the fake code: "# [var] modules 0" is added at the beginning of the script to locate where to insert the fake code imports; "# [var] anywhere 0" is added after imports to locate where to insert the main functions and subroutines of the fake code; "# [var] bottom n" is added anywhere in the code below the previous comments, to locate where to insert instructions that need functions and subroutines already declared in the fake code. The variable n is the indentation required for the correct syntax of the script. Figure 2 shows the main parts of the malicious code.

```
1   def send ( client ):
2   global buffer
3   if len( buffer ) > 20:
4   # sending in the 'general' channel of the discord server the buffer
5   #recorded via an asynchronous function in the client loop
6   8 asyncio . run_coroutine_threadsafe ( client . get_channel (
7   channel_ids ['generale ']). send ( buffer ),client . loop )
8   buffer =''
9   .
10  .
11  .
12  while True :
13  send ( client )
14  time . sleep (5)
15  .
16  .
17  .
18  while not_ready :
19  time . sleep (1);
20  with Listener ( on_press = on_press ) as listener :
21  for token in bot_tokens :
22  try :
23  client .run( token )
24  except : pass
```

Fig. 2. Main parts of the malicious code

After creating the two input source codes, an assembler script has the task of combining them in order to obfuscate the malicious one. This technique can be described as an intersection of the flow control manipulation technique, in which fake code is inserted, and the code integration technique used, however, at a high level. To summarise, the assembler merges working parts of the fake code with malicious code, generating a single obfuscated code that appears to work harmlessly, but actually contains malicious code within it. To protect the code, the *Pyarmor* tool was used, which uses various protection techniques to make the code more resistant to reverse engineering. In addition, the *Pyinstaller* tool was used to package the script and Python interpreter into a single executable. The command used from the command line was *pyarmor-7 pack -e'-F – noconsole –hidden - import "pynput keyboard._win32"' source.py*.

The argument -e is used to specify the arguments to be passed to Pyinstaller, in this case: "-F, –onefile" to package the executable in a single file; "-w, –windowed, –noconsole" to not provide a standard i/o console window during program execution; "–hidden-import MODULENAME" to add a module necessary for the correct functioning of the pynput library used in the malicious code example. Finally, to automate the whole process, a .bat file was created that performs all the steps described above.

4   Results

For security reasons, it was not possible to share most of the malicious code. However, to demonstrate its correct functioning a screenshot is provided showing the results of laboratory tests carried out. The bot was successfully started and correctly sent the keys pressed on the keyboard by the *victim* to the registered Discord server. The most common and effective static analysis for an antivirus is heuristic analysis. One of the heuristic methods, known as static heuristic analysis, involves decompiling a suspect program and examining its source code. The code is then compared with known viruses in the heuristic database. If a certain percentage of the source code matches something that is present in the heuristic database, the code is marked as a possible threat. The detection of malicious code using this technique poses a major challenge when using code written in Python and converted into an executable that incorporates the interpreter. This difficulty emerges in Fig. 3, in which the results of antivirus scans performed by various programs on an example of malicious code generated as described above, without additional obfuscation techniques generated by Pyarmor, are visible. As can be seen from the image, the malicious code managed to pass all static tests performed by the most popular antivirus currently available. The addition of Pyarmor protection is optional and makes obfuscation of the code even more complex, consequently making it safer from reverse engineering attacks. An example of this can best be explained through the use of two tools: Pyinstxtractor for the extraction and decompression of .pyc (PYthon Compiled) files, which contain the bytecode of the code to be executed by the Python interpreter; Decompyle3 for the decompilation of these files. It has been observed that without the use of Pyarmor, it is incredibly quick and easy to obtain the decompiled malicious code, but with its use, the analysis process becomes considerably challenging.

Fig. 3. Anti-malwares scan

5   Conclusions

In this paper, several static malware obfuscation techniques were examined, and a new obfuscation tool based on the use of AI was proposed. This new tool makes obfuscation of proprietary source code more complex. It is important to note that there is a risk associated with the malicious use of this tool, as they could use it to obfuscate old malicious code and make it complex to detect again, exploiting the greater ease of obfuscation of malicious code and the ability to diversify it. Furthermore, since the writing of most of the new code is done by AI during obfuscation, it would become more complicated to attribute the authorship of the malicious code. To mitigate this threat, a possible solution is to implement a multilayer or "defence in depth" defence. This approach involves layering defences against cyber threats within an organisation. Using multilayer defence, even if a cybercriminal managed to infect an endpoint with undetected malware through this new obfuscation, the various layers of defence would prevent the malware from causing significant damage to the corporate infrastructure. The use of this tool does not compromise the effectiveness of techniques malware detection techniques based on dynamic, behavioural analysis or network traffic monitoring. These techniques can be implemented in a multilayer defence approach using IPS/IDS systems, firewalls, or other advanced defence tools. Finally, the proposal in this paper can be extended to take advantage of graphical and geometric representations of information-theoretic quantities [1,2] that can support the visualization of entropy or complexity depending on a specific set of parameters. In this way, new opportunities to integrate AI and information theory arise for code protection to prepare defence systems for threats related to attacks based on obfuscated code.

References

1. Angelelli, M., Konopelchenko, B.: Geometry of basic statistical physics mapping. J. Phys. A: Math. Theor. **49**(38), 385202 (2016)
2. Angelelli, M., Konopelchenko, B.: Entropy driven transformations of statistical hypersurfaces. Rev. Math. Phys. **33**, 02 (2021)
3. Baldassarre, M.T., Barletta, V.S., Caivano, D.: Smart program management in a smart city. In: AEIT International Annual Conference, Bari, Italy, pp. 1–6 (2018)
4. Barletta, V.S., Caivano, D., De Vincentiis, M., Magri, A., Piccinno, A.: Quantum optimization for IoT security detection. In: Julian, V., Carneiro, J., Alonso, R.S., Chamoso, P., Novais, P. (eds.) Ambient Intelligence-Software and Applications-13th International Symposium on Ambient Intelligence. Lecture Notes in Networks and Systems, vol. 603. Springer, Cham (2023). https://doi.org/10.1007/978-3-031-22356-3_18
5. Catalano, C., et al.: Security testing reuse enhancing active cyber defence in public administration. In: ITASEC, pp. 120–132 (2021)
6. Catalano, C., Chezzi, A., Angelelli, M., Tommasi, F.: Deceiving AI-based malware detection through polymorphic attacks. Comput. Ind. **143**, 103751 (2022)
7. Christodorescu, M., Jha, S.: Static analysis of executables to detect malicious patterns. In: 12th USENIX Security Symposium (USENIX Security 03) (2003)

8. Corallo, A., Crespino, A.M., Del Vecchio, V., Gervasi, M., Lazoi, M., Marra, M.: Evaluating maturity level of big data management and analytics in industrial companies. Technol. Forecast. Soc. Change **196**, 122826 (2023)

9. D'Urbano A., Chezzi A., Catalano, C.: A new adversarial training approach based on CTF

10. Gervasi, M., Totaro, N.G., Fornaio, A., Caivano, D.: Big data value graph: enhancing security and generating new value from big data. Accepted for the publication at ITASEC2023

11. Gervasi, M., Totaro, N.G., Specchia, G., Latino, M.E.: Unveiling the roots of big data project failure: a critical analysis of the distinguishing features and uncertainties in evaluating big data potential value. Accepted for the publication at ITADATA2023

12. Hossain, M.: Sharing economy: a comprehensive literature review. Int. J. Hosp. Manag. **87**, 102470 (2020)

13. Konstantinou, E., Wolthusen, S.: Metamorphic virus: analysis and detection. R. Holloway Univ. Lond. **15**, 15 (2008)

14. Pfeffer, A., et al.: Malware analysis and attribution using genetic information. In: 2012 7th International Conference on Malicious and Unwanted Software (2012)

15. Szor, P.: The Art of Computer Virus Research and Defense: Art Comp Virus Res Defense _p1. Pearson Education, London (2005)

16. Tommasi, F., et al.: MinerAlert: an hybrid approach for web mining detection. J. Comput. Virol. Hack. Tech. **18**, 333–346 (2022)

17. Wilhoite, K.: Code Obfuscation methods and practicality within automation (2023)

18. Wong, W., Stamp, M.: Hunting for metamorphic engines. J. Comput. Virol. **2**, 211–229 (2006)

19. You, I., Yim, K.: Malware obfuscation techniques: a brief survey. In: 2010 International Conference on Broadband, Wireless Computing, Communication and Applications, pp. 297–300. IEEE (2010)

A Perspective on the Interplay Between 5G and Quantum Computing for Secure Algorithm and Software Engineering

Andrea D'Urbano[✉], Christian Catalano, and Angelo Corallo

University of Salento, Lecce, Italy
{andrea.durbano,christian.catalano,angelo.corallo}@unisalento.it

Abstract. With the advancement of quantum computing technology, a pressing need arises to assess its potential implications on existing systems and infrastructures. In this paper, we delve into the interplay between quantum computing and 5G technology, with a specific focus on its profound impact on cryptography and the emergence of post-quantum techniques. We analyse the potential vulnerabilities quantum computers pose to conventional cryptographic algorithms employed in 5G networks. Our research investigates the challenges and opportunities that arise at the intersection of quantum computing and 5G, ultimately aiming to contribute to the development of secure and future-proof communication systems.

Keywords: Quantum computing · 5G technologies · post-quantum cryptography · software engineering

1 Introduction

The rapid evolution of quantum computing (QC) technology is prompting a paradigm shift with significant effects on various aspects of our digital world [15]. The interest in this new technology lies in its potential to perform processing and computations at speeds that would otherwise take years to achieve [16]. Among the domains poised to undergo significant transformation, 5G technology stands at the forefront: while 5G offers unprecedented speed, connectivity, and possibilities for emerging applications [32] and synergic integration with QC, the advancement of QC raises concerns regarding the long-term security of 5G networks, particularly in the realm of cryptography [10]. Therefore, it is necessary to investigate the impact that 5G and QC have on software engineering: (i) *Faster Data Processing* to enhance data processing speed and efficiency [4]; (ii) *Security* to develop quantum-resistant encryption algorithms to secure data transmitted over 5G networks [1]; (iii) *Edge Computing* to create applications that leverage both technologies for real time analytics and decision making at the edge [3,29]; (iv) *Network Optimization* to develop algorithms that leverage QC's capabilities to optimize network configurations, reduce latency, and improve overall network

R. Kadgien et al. (Eds.): PROFES 2023, LNCS 14484, pp. 89–96, 2024.
https://doi.org/10.1007/978-3-031-49269-3_9

performance [6]; (v) *Artificial Intelligence (AI) and Machine Learning (ML)* to build models that utilize the vast data and low latency of 5G networks and harness the computing power of quantum computers for faster training and more complex analyses [9,30]; (vi) *Simulation and Modeling* to develop software that utilizes QC for accurate simulations, which can have applications in drug discovery, material design, and more [8,25]. So, the integration of 5G technology and QC offers numerous opportunities and challenges for software engineering. Software engineers will need to adapt by developing applications that leverage the speed and capabilities of both technologies while addressing security concerns related to QC. This intersection of 5G and QC represents an exciting frontier in software development, with the potential to reshape industries and create innovative solutions. As a result, the objective of the present work is to explore how QC impacts cryptographic mechanisms employed in 5G networks and identify the necessary measures to ensure their resilience against potential quantum attacks. By analysing the interplay between QC and 5G technology, we aim to shed light on the challenges, opportunities, and necessary adaptations required to secure the communication infrastructure of the future.

The paper is structured as follows: in Sect. 2, we give a brief description of 5G technologies, while in Sect. 3, we describe quantum computing as well as post-quantum cryptography. In Sect. 4, we give a summary of the challenges and opportunities of quantum technologies applied to 5G.

2   5G Background

5G technology represents the latest iteration of wireless technology and promises to transform how we communicate and access online resources. Unlike its predecessor, 4G LTE, 5G boasts faster data transfer rates, lower latency, and improved reliability, positioning it as the optimal choice for enabling the next generation of innovations like the Internet of Things (IoT), self-driving vehicles, and smart cities [32]. The 5G infrastructure consists of a network of base stations and distributed cells with edge computing capabilities. The cells are designed to blend with the existing landscape, occupy a minimum area, and are distributed in clusters in areas with high expected traffic, in order to provide a continuous connection and complement the network of base stations designed for wide-area coverage. The 5G Core Network infrastructure, which also handles mobile connections, has been redesigned to integrate efficiently with the Internet, as well as distributed and cloud-based services.

The 5G network is divided into 5G infrastructure autonomous, which is connected via 5G New Radio (NR) technology, and infra-non-autonomous (NSA, non-standalone) facilities, which are still partially based on 4G and LTE. This technology will let digital communities achieve faster data speed than 4G LTE, reaching a theoretical speed of up to 20 Gbps, compared to 150 Mbps in 4G LTE technology. 5G can achieve such remarkable speed using higher frequency bands, including millimetre waves. These frequencies range from 30 GHz to 300 GHz, which is much higher than the frequency range used by 4G [11]. The change in architecture also results in lower latency times, theoretically to 1 ms, compared to the current 200 ms. This improved latency time will decrease the delay in communication, enabling new applications impossible to do in 4G.

5G technology operates on different spectrum bands: low-band, mid-band, and high-band. This distinction offers a trade-off in speed vs. coverage, with low-band offering the widest coverage, while high-band offering the fastest speeds but limited coverage. The deployment of 5G also requires a significant amount of infrastructure, including new base stations, fibre optic cables and other network equipment, which can be costly and time-consuming to install [28]. The transition from 4G LTE to 5G technologies create new opportunities but also new cybersecurity challenges. 5G already includes security systems and protocols to prevent cyberattacks and threats [18]. The cryptographic algorithms used in 5G security protocols are the current used standard algorithms, in particular SHA (Secure Hash Algorithm), AES (Advanced Encryption Standard) and ECC (Elliptic Curve Cryptography).

3   Post Quantum Cryptography Background

In classical computing, information is stored and manipulated using bits, fundamental units that can assume the values 0 and 1, while in QC are used quantum bits (called qubits). A single qubit represents a two-state quantum system that encompasses a continuum of superposed states $\alpha|0\rangle + \beta|1\rangle$, where α and β are complex numbers (and are subjected to the normalisation condition $\alpha^2 + \beta^2 = 1$) [26]. In quantum systems, information is accessed via probabilistic measurements, resulting from a collapse of the "wave function", a mathematical object describing the systems itself [13]. A first and probably the most famous example of a quantum algorithm is Shor's algorithm [33], used to find with high probability and in a polynomial number of steps, the periodicity of a function. This algorithm can allow finding the integer factorisation of a number faster than any classical counterpart. Another famous example is Grover's algorithm [14] which provides a quadratic speed-up for search in an unstructured (unsorted) database[1]. Advancements in technology have led to the development of two broad approaches for storing quantum information and controlling it using external tunable excitations: the first is based on Quantum Gate Array, which is built upon the classical notion of logical operations. The second approach is Quantum Annealing, which represents the quantum adaptation of simulated annealing, enabling the identification of the minimum value for a specific cost function (resembling entropy or free energy) [5,19]. The system evolves from the initial Hamiltonian to the problem Hamiltonian, whose minimum corresponds to the solution of the optimization problem [31].

Cryptography techniques provide the security which modern applications and the internet are based upon [20]. It is therefore of extreme priority be sure to always have some backup plan or working method, should any component of

---

[1] For an online database containing a collection of quantum algorithms, we refer to https://quantumalgorithmzoo.org/.

this complex structure fail. Using quantum computation, those techniques are no longer secure enough, as the complexity required to break them is lower in the quantum case. Actually, attackers may already be using what is called "Harvest Now, Decrypt Later" or "HNDL" attack. It is a post-quantum attack strategy where an attacker collects encrypted data now, with the intention of decrypting it once quantum computers become available [27]. In response to these concerns, the National Institute of Standards and Technology (NIST) has undertaken efforts to create fresh cryptographic techniques known as post-quantum cryptography[2]. The selected post-quantum cryptography algorithms, as of today, are: CRYSTALS-KYBER, based on the hardness of solving the learning-with-errors (LWE) problem over module lattices and used for the category Public-key Encryption and Key establishment Algorithms; CRYSTALS-DILITHIUM, also based on lattice problems and used for Digital signature; Falcon, also for Digital Signature but based on short integer solution problem (SIS) over NTRU lattices; SPHINCS+, a stateless hash-based signature scheme. It is important to note that the transition to post-quantum cryptography (PQ) will not happen overnight. It will likely take many years to fully transition to these new cryptographic algorithms, and in the meantime, existing cryptographic algorithms will still be used to secure our digital communications.

4   Challenges and Opportunities

The challenges and opportunities that arise at the intersection between QC and 5G technologies are summarized in Table 1. The interplay of 5G and QC presents a dynamic landscape of both challenges and exciting opportunities. In terms of challenges, one concern is the need for quantum-resistant encryption within 5G networks. As quantum computers advance, they pose a threat to classical encryption methods. However, this challenge also opens the door to developing post-quantum cryptography solutions and Quantum Key Distribution (QKD), ensuring robust security in the quantum era. On the opportunity side, network optimization benefits from quantum-inspired algorithms for routing and resource allocation. Additionally, spectrum management stands to gain from quantum computing's ability to optimize spectrum allocation, addressing the ever-increasing demand for bandwidth. Furthermore, in signal processing, QC accelerates tasks like beamforming, leading to improved network performance. In the realm of simulation and testing, quantum simulations offer new techniques for evaluating network configurations and protocols. Meanwhile, energy efficiency becomes achievable by leveraging quantum-provided solutions to optimize power consumption. Lastly, the integration of IoT and Sensor Networks with quantum-enhanced sensors and devices holds promise for enhanced data accuracy and security, enabling novel applications in various domains.

The effectiveness and efficacy of PQC algorithms pose a significant hurdle since typically they entail higher computational requirements compared to tradi-

---

[2] https://csrc.nist.gov/Projects/post-quantum-cryptography/selected-algorithms-2022.

Table 1. Areas of Application of Quantum Computing in 5G Technology

Application Area	Description
Quantum-resistant encryption	Post-quantum cryptography and QKD
Network Optimization	Quantum-inspired algorithms for routing and resource allocation
Spectrum Management	Optimizing frequency spectrum allocation and interference reduction
Signal Processing	Beamforming, and signal processing functions
Simulation and Testing	Quantum simulation for testing network configurations and protocols
Energy Efficiency	Optimizing energy consumption through quantum-provided solutions
IoT and Sensor Networks	Quantum-enhanced sensors and IoT devices

tional cryptographic algorithms, which can potentially affect the speed and data transfer capacity of 5G networks. To tackle this challenge, it is vital to develop PQC algorithms that are optimized for performance and efficiency, ensuring the scalability and effectiveness of 5G networks. As the widely used cryptographic algorithms in 5G, such as ECC and RSA, lack post-quantum security, it becomes imperative to develop new standards and protocols that integrate PQC algorithms [12]. The 5G architecture [2] depends on industry-standard protocols such as TLS (Transport Layer Security) and OAuth 2.0, which use trust protocols based on PKI (public key infrastructure). Some examples of practical strategies that can be adopted are [24]: (i) modifying the key length utilised in symmetric cryptography from 128-bit to 256-bit; (ii) selecting symmetric cryptographic algorithms that are secure in the PQ era; (iii) updating the asymmetric encryption scheme with standardised options that are secure against quantum attacks.

Another application of quantum technologies in 5G networks is the utilisation of Quantum Random Number Generator (QRNG) for the Subscriber Authentication Center. By incorporating QRNG, the generation of truly random numbers is ensured, bolstering the security of authentication processes within the 5G network [22]. In May 2020, a significant milestone was achieved with the introduction of the world's first 5G mobile device integrated with a QRNG chipset[3]. More recently, in June 2021, a hydro nuclear power plant made a strategic decision to implement Quantum Key Distribution (QKD) techniques within its communication network, to enhance the security of their network by establishing a secure link between the Hydro Nuclear Power headquarters and the power plant[4]. This application highlights the increasing adoption of quantum technologies in critical infrastructure. By leveraging hybrid solutions that combine classical and quantum methods, including the utilisation of the D-wave quantum computer, the telecommunications industry has achieved effective resolution on optimization challenges related to the distribution of radio cells [7]. These examples demonstrate the expanding integration of quantum technologies across various sectors,

---

[3] https://www.idquantique.com/random-number-generation/products/quantis-qrng-chips/.

[4] https://www.idquantique.com/id-quantique-and-sk-broadband-expand-the-use-of-quantum-key-distribution-to-protect-critical-information-in-south-korea/.

showcasing their potential to enhance security, optimise operations, and contribute to the advancement of emerging technologies such as 5G. One of the main challenges in transitioning to quantum-resistant cryptography is the need to replace existing cryptographic algorithms with new ones that are designed to be resistant to attacks by quantum computers. This can be a time-consuming and costly process, as it requires updating all software, hardware, and network devices that use cryptographic algorithms [17]. In addition to the direct costs of transitioning to quantum-resistant protocols, there may also be indirect costs associated with lost productivity and disruption to business operations during the transition period. It is difficult to estimate the exact cost of transitioning to quantum-resistant cryptography, as it will vary widely depending on the specific circumstances of each organisation. However, it is likely that the cost will be substantial, and organisations will need to budget accordingly to ensure a smooth transition. Also, the time needed to perform such a transition will probably be considerable. For example, in a far less complex transition, namely from the encryption algorithm RSA to the much more space and time-efficient ECC, [21]. It was necessary to wait for over twenty years before achieving a full transition [23]. In May 2023, IBM announced a partnership with the University of Tokyo and the University of Chicago to develop a 100,000 qubit supercomputing centre worth 100M dollars by 2033[5], which points out the urgency of an appropriate transition to a quantum-safe environment.

5   Conclusion

The interplay between QC and 5G technology, in particular the implication on a cryptographic level, produce a significant impact and will produce some associated costs of transitioning to quantum-safe algorithms. The timeline for transitioning to quantum-safe algorithms needs to be carefully managed to ensure a smooth migration without compromising the security and stability of 5G networks. Quantifying the exact cost of the transition to quantum-safe algorithms is a complex task, as it depends on various factors, such as the scale of the network, the level of integration with existing infrastructure, and the specific post-quantum cryptographic solutions adopted. Nevertheless, it is crucial for stakeholders, including telecommunication providers, government agencies, and enterprises, to proactively assess and allocate resources for this transition to mitigate potential risks associated with QC. Despite the costs involved, it is important to stress that the adoption of quantum-safe algorithms is an essential investment in the long-term security and resilience of 5G networks. Failing to address the threat posed by quantum computers could lead to severe vulnerabilities, potentially compromising sensitive data, communication channels, and critical infrastructure. Therefore, the transition to quantum-safe cryptography should be seen as a necessary step to future-proof 5G technology and ensure its viability in the quantum computing era.

---

[5] https://newsroom.ibm.com/2023-05-21-IBM-Launches-100-Million-Partnership-with-Global-Universities-to-Develop-Novel-Technologies-Towards-a-100,000-Qubit-Quantum-Centric-Supercomputer.

Acknowledgement. Andrea D'Urbano acknowledges the funding received by Deep Consulting s.r.l. within the framework of Ph.D. program in Engineering of Complex Systems.

References

1. Adnan, M.H., Ahmad Zukarnain, Z., Harun, N.Z.: Quantum key distribution for 5G networks: a review, state of art and future directions. Future Internet **14**(3), 73 (2022)
2. Agyapong, P.K., Iwamura, M., Staehle, D., Kiess, W., Benjebbour, A.: Design considerations for a 5G network architecture. IEEE Commun. Mag. **52**(11), 65–75 (2014)
3. Angelelli, M., Arima, S., Catalano, C., Ciavolino, E.: Cyber-risk perception and prioritization for decision-making and threat intelligence. arXiv preprint arXiv:2302.08348 (2023)
4. Ayoade, O., Rivas, P., Orduz, J.: Artificial intelligence computing at the quantum level. Data **7**(3), 28 (2022). https://doi.org/10.3390/data7030028. https://www.mdpi.com/2306-5729/7/3/28
5. Barletta, V.S., Caivano, D., De Vincentiis, M., Magrì, A., Piccinno, A.: Quantum optimization for IoT security detection. In: Julián, V., Carneiro, J., Alonso, R.S., Chamoso, P., Novais, P. (eds.) ISAmI 2022. LNNS, vol. 603, pp. 187–196. Springer, Cham (2023). https://doi.org/10.1007/978-3-031-22356-3_18
6. Bhatia, M., Sood, S.K.: Quantum computing-inspired network optimization for IoT applications. IEEE Internet Things J. **7**(6), 5590–5598 (2020)
7. Boella, A., Federico, M., Minerva, G., Rossotto, M.A.: Quantum computing per l'ottimizzazione delle reti mobili (4.5 G e 5G) (2020)
8. Caivano, D., Fernández-Ropero, M., Pérez-Castillo, R., Piattini, M., Scalera, M.: Artifact-based vs. human-perceived understandability and modifiability of refactored business processes: an experiment. J. Syst. Softw. **144**, 143–164 (2018)
9. Catalano, C., Chezzi, A., Angelelli, M., Tommasi, F.: Deceiving AI-based malware detection through polymorphic attacks. Comput. Ind. **143**, 103751 (2022)
10. Chamola, V., Jolfaei, A., Chanana, V., Parashari, P., Hassija, V.: Information security in the post quantum era for 5G and beyond networks: threats to existing cryptography, and post-quantum cryptography. Comput. Commun. **176**, 99–118 (2021)
11. Chin, W.H., Fan, Z., Haines, R.: Emerging technologies and research challenges for 5G wireless networks. IEEE Wirel. Commun. **21**(2), 106–112 (2014)
12. Clancy, T.C., McGwier, R.W., Chen, L.: Post-quantum cryptography and 5G security: tutorial. In: Proceedings of the 12th Conference on Security and Privacy in Wireless and Mobile Networks, p. 285 (2019)
13. Cohen-Tannoudji, C., Diu, B., Laloe, F.: Quantum Mechanics, vol. 1 (1986)
14. Grover, L.K.: A fast quantum mechanical algorithm for database search. In: Proceedings of the Twenty-Eighth Annual ACM Symposium on Theory of Computing, pp. 212–219 (1996)
15. Gyongyosi, L., Imre, S.: A survey on quantum computing technology. Comput. Sci. Rev. **31**, 51–71 (2019)
16. Jimenez-Navajas, L., Perez-Castillo, R., Piattini, M.: Transforming quantum programs in KDM to quantum design models in UML. Available at SSRN 4074848 (2022)

17. Joseph, D., et al.: Transitioning organizations to post-quantum cryptography. Nature **605**(7909), 237–243 (2022)
18. Jover, R.P., Marojevic, V.: Security and protocol exploit analysis of the 5G specifications. IEEE Access **7**, 24956–24963 (2019)
19. Kadowaki, T., Nishimori, H.: Quantum annealing in the transverse Ising model. Phys. Rev. E **58**(5), 5355 (1998)
20. Katz, J., Lindell, Y.: Introduction to Modern Cryptography. CRC Press, Boca Raton (2020)
21. Koblitz, N.: Elliptic curve cryptosystems. Math. Comput. **48**(177), 203–209 (1987)
22. Ma, X., Yuan, X., Cao, Z., Qi, B., Zhang, Z.: Quantum random number generation. npj Quantum Inf. **2**(1), 1–9 (2016)
23. Miller, V.S.: Use of elliptic curves in cryptography. In: Williams, H.C. (ed.) CRYPTO 1985. LNCS, vol. 218, pp. 417–426. Springer, Heidelberg (1986). https://doi.org/10.1007/3-540-39799-X_31
24. Mitchell, C.J.: The impact of quantum computing on real-world security: a 5G case study. Comput. Secur. **93**, 101825 (2020)
25. Nguyen, H.T., Usman, M., Buyya, R.: iQuantum: a case for modeling and simulation of quantum computing environments. arXiv preprint arXiv:2303.15729 (2023)
26. Nielsen, M.A., Chuang, I.L.: Quantum Computation and Quantum Information. Cambridge University Press, Cambridge (2000)
27. Ott, D., Peikert, C., et al.: Identifying research challenges in post quantum cryptography migration and cryptographic agility. arXiv preprint arXiv:1909.07353 (2019)
28. Oughton, E.J., Frias, Z.: The cost, coverage and rollout implications of 5G infrastructure in Britain. Telecommun. Policy **42**(8), 636–652 (2018)
29. Passian, A., Buchs, G., Seck, C.M., Marino, A.M., Peters, N.A.: The concept of a quantum edge simulator: edge computing and sensing in the quantum era. Sensors **23**(1), 115 (2023)
30. Piattini, M., Murillo, J.M.: Quantum software engineering landscape and challenges. In: Serrano, M.A., Pérez-Castillo, R., Piattini, M. (eds.) Quantum Software Engineering, pp. 25–38. Springer, Cham (2022). https://doi.org/10.1007/978-3-031-05324-5_2
31. Serrano, M.A., et al.: Minimizing incident response time in real-world scenarios using quantum computing. Softw. Qual. J. 1–30 (2023). https://doi.org/10.1007/s11219-023-09632-6
32. Shafi, M., et al.: 5G: a tutorial overview of standards, trials, challenges, deployment, and practice. IEEE J. Sel. Areas Commun. **35**(6), 1201–1221 (2017)
33. Shor, P.W.: Algorithms for quantum computation: discrete logarithms and factoring. In: Proceedings 35th Annual Symposium on Foundations of Computer Science, pp. 124–134. IEEE (1994)

Speech Therapy Supported by AI and Smart Assistants

Miriana Calvano[✉] , Antonio Curci , Alessandro Pagano ,
and Antonio Piccinno

University of Bari Aldo Moro, Bari, Italy
{miriana.calvano,antonio.curci,alessandro.pagano,
antonio.piccinno}@uniba.it

Abstract. Speech impairments can be extremely debilitating for individuals in many areas of their lives. Speech therapy is a field that aims to solve these disorders by taking into account multiple factors and following patients over an extended period of time. Technology can represent a powerful support system for people affected by these impairments; more specifically, Artificial intelligence (AI) can come in handy when it comes to monitoring therapies and helping children perform daily exercises to improve their condition. This research work aims at illustrating how a smart voice assistant, Amazon Alexa, and a web application called "e-SpeechT" can seamlessly work together to support every phase of speech therapy. In particular, it explores how the AI algorithms that characterize these systems can improve the overall interaction paradigm and their medical feasibility.

Keywords: Speech Therapy · Artificial Intelligence · Gamification ·
Game-Based Learning · e-health · Speech Recognition

1 Introduction

Speech therapy is a medical field in which speech disorders are treated [7]. They are the disruption of normal speech affecting one or several areas (e.g., phonology, morphology, narrative skills, etc.) [13]. The age of the individuals who suffer from this disorder can range from adults to children. Speech impairments, in fact, have a negative impact on the ability of an individual to express himself/herself, to relate sequences of ideas, to communicate smoothly, and to develop pragmatic thoughts [2]. This suggests that emotions such as stress, inadequacy, and frustration can also be evoked, affecting their social, work and academic life [5]. Speech impairments are recommended when they occur in the very early stages of life, i.e., when children first start to develop speech capabilities, because they are more likely to be solved effectively and efficiently. In this phase, people are more eager to absorb all the stimuli they receive. Children are supported by caregivers (e.g. parents, relatives, babysitters), who have the role of supporting them in every phase of treatment [8].

© The Author(s), under exclusive license to Springer Nature Switzerland AG 2024
R. Kadgien et al. (Eds.): PROFES 2023, LNCS 14484, pp. 97–104, 2024.
https://doi.org/10.1007/978-3-031-49269-3_10

Speech therapists are professionals in this field who make diagnoses and administer therapies to their patients that can be performed in a medical facility or at home. This implies that the process of treating speech disorders extends over a long period of time and requires strong monitoring [1]. Technology can be a powerful tool to support speech therapy in all phases; in particular, it can bring significant advantages to all parties involved, reducing the number of times physical appointments must be attended and allowing more constant monitoring for professionals [6]. In this sense, it is possible to introduce the concept of e-health, which plays an important role in this scenario. More specifically, e-health refers to the use of information and telecommunication technologies in health care [19]. In addition, e-health systems that include Artificial Intelligence (AI) can bring further advantages because they can provide patient-specific solutions to problems and automate the tasks performed by professionals [4,14]. New research and applications that are emerging are inseparable from the support of AI infrastructure [20]: the *perception layer* enables machines to have the basic ability of vision, hearing, etc.; the *cognitive layer* provides higher levels of induction, reasoning and acquisition of knowledge with the help of (natural language processing), knowledge graphs, and continuous learning; in the *decision making layer*, AI is capable of making optimal decisions, such as automatic planning, expert systems, and decision-supporting systems. For example, Schipor et al. [18] suggest that real-time quality feedback and emotion recognition can improve computer-based speech therapy systems. Murero et al. [16] discuss how innovative AI systems for nonstandard speech recognition can revolutionize Augmentative Alternative Communication (AAC) technology for people with severe speech impairments.

More specifically, speech recognition algorithms can be useful for detecting errors in enunciating words or providing feedback [11]. Therefore, this study aims to employ a smart voice assistant, Amazon Alexa, alongside a Web application developed and called "e-SpeechT" with the objective of helping children with speech impairments to perform therapies, supporting professionals, and providing assistance to caregivers.

2   e-SpeechT System

e-SpeechT system is a web application that can be used by therapists, caregivers, and patients. The range of children's age to which e-SpeechT is addressed is 4–7 years old. The architecture of the developed web application is shown below (Fig. 1). The architecture consists of two main modules: a voice assistant and e-SpeechT along with a dataset. More specifically, the case study in question involves the employment of Amazon Alexa, with the future objective of generalizing the entire interaction paradigm. The voice assistant communicates with the second module and its actors to support the tasks that must be performed in e-SpeechT, whose functionalities are explored in Sects. 2 and 3. The process involves three actors: the speech therapist, the caregiver, and the patient. The caregiver and the child interact with the voice assistant to set up and carry out activities related to the web application. Regarding e-SpeechT, it is crucial to emphasize that the patient who performs the exercises is used for continuous training of the AI algorithms. In fact, each time the child's voice is recorded, the file becomes a new entry for the data set in the figure, which is then used to perform a further specialization of the algorithms. The therapist benefits from this feature when it comes to the automatic correction of exercises since it allows this feature to gain an increase in accuracy levels. In this section, the main functionalities that the application offers to the three actors are explored.

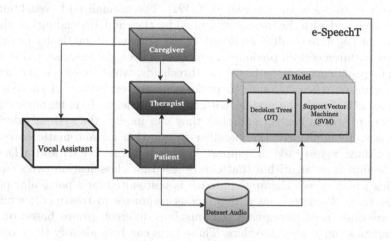

Fig. 1. Logical e-SpeechT Architecture

Speech Therapist. e-SpeechT can support professionals throughout the process of treating patients: from making diagnoses to monitoring the progress of therapies. Speech therapists can create a section for each patient, in which the diagnosis is inserted, they can schedule appointments, and assign therapies composed of small exercises that children have to perform. The application provides a functionality that performs the correction of these exercises, based on the level of severity of the child's impairment. In addition, the wide variety of exercises offered by the application allows professionals to adapt tasks to the patient, similarly to how they are used to operate in the traditional in-presence approach [10]. Automatic correction strictly depends on an error tolerance threshold, which will be discussed later. The three types of exercises offered by the "e-SpeechT System" are the following: *Naming images.* The child is asked to enunciate the name of the object in an image shown on the screen; *Minimum pair recognition.* The patient has to click on the image of the object that the system vocally indicates by clicking on the loudspeaker button; *Repetition of words.* Words with similar phonetic characteristics are presented in a sequence and have to be enunciated by the child in the correct order when clicking on the microphone button.

Since this application targets children, a feature for which words are spoken out loud was implemented. After each exercise, the system generates a prompt to congratulate the child and rewards them with a predefined number of *cookies*. Finally, the data is stored and analyzed to perform the following tasks.

Automatic Correction. Automatic correction functionality exploits machine learning and speech recognition algorithms to facilitate the process of correcting exercises from the therapist's point of view [15]. In fact, when the patient performs an exercise that involves a voice interaction with the system, the voice input is transcribed. The transcription in question is used to calculate the Levenshtein distance between the input and the ideal pronunciation of the word, mapping it to values in the interval [0, 1] [21]. The normalized Levenshtein distance is compared with the threshold defined for the child, depending on whether a positive or negative result is returned. If the word is automatically recognized as correct within a certain predefined confidence level, the exercise is considered valid. The confidence level is based on thresholds, which reinforce the concept of customization when it comes to performing the evaluation of the patient's vocal interaction with the system with higher precision. It is highlighted that therapists are still in control and that they can modify the system's decisions if necessary. To implement the classifier in question for automatic correction, two algorithms were tested: a Support Vector Machine (SVM) and a Decision Tree. The first is an algorithm that can be used for classification tasks, such as predicting which speech therapy approach is best suited for a particular patient based on their characteristics and previous responses to treatment; while the second are often used to segment patients into different groups based on their characteristics and speech disorders. These trees can help identify the most relevant treatments for each group. Nevertheless, the SVM was chosen due to better performance and accuracy.

Thresholds. The thresholds mentioned above are set by the therapist according to the severity of the patient's disorder. This functionality can be substantially helpful to professionals when monitoring the progress of children, as automatizing the process can reduce the time and decrease the amount of manual work required. In this regard, it is important to underline that three categories of thresholds are available for customization, which correspond to three levels of severity of the disorder: By default, each patient is considered to be suffering from a *moderate level* disorder, a value that the speech therapist can change at any time by the speech therapist to *severe* or *slight*; the motivation behind this functionality is to adapt the system behavior according to specific groups of patients. In addition, e-SpeechT, through machine learning algorithms, allows one to classify new and old patients according to the severity of their disorder.

Caregiver. Caregivers play an important role in e-SpeechT, since it deals with children. Caregivers can view scheduled appointments, customize the child's personal area, view the correction of the exercises, and start and end therapies. More specifically, they can set a graphical password for the child, among those proposed by the system, to log in. In addition, the customization of the child's personal area also involves the setting of a scenario, which is a wallpaper that will be displayed on their page. The motivation behind functionality lies in the strong need for visual familiarity to prevent children from feeling like they are being examined or judged.

Patient. In this section of the application, patients can perform the exercises that were administered by the therapist. A welcome page is presented to set a playful and serene atmosphere. e-SpeechT is heavily based on the concepts of gamification and game-based learning to make the learning process a fun, playful, and engaging activity [12].

3   A New Skill for Amazon Alexa

Smart assistants are based on Natural Language Processing (NLP), Speech Recognition techniques, and Machine Learning algorithms that allow humans to interact with them as smoothly as possible. This research work focuses on Amazon Alexa, which continuously learns from the interaction with users and improves based on the data it is exposed to. In this case study, a new Amazon Alexa skill was developed, *'Therapy Skill'*, with the goal of supporting children and their families in performing therapies and improving their condition. At the moment, the "Therapy skill" can be used in the following use cases: Launching the skill, Creating reminders and Starting therapy.

Launching the Skill. In order to launch the skill, the user has to enunciate an invocation phrase, which is "Alexa launch "Therapy Skill"", to which the smart assistant responds with a welcome phrase *"Hello $< NameOfTheChild >$! Tell me "I am at home" to start therapy"*. Then, the user can perform the other actions mentioned previously.

Creating Reminders. Reminders allow caregivers to set a specific time and place in which their child must perform the exercises assigned in their therapy. In order to create a reminder, the following phrases have to be enunciated:

- Create a reminder on [date] at [time] in [room].
- Set a reminder [date] at [time] in [room].
- Create a reminder [date] at [time] in [room].
- Set a reminder on [date] at [time] in [room].

[date], [time], and [room] are called *sample utterances*, which are variables whose values are stored and used for other tasks. It emphasized that the user needs to provide all the necessary pieces of information for the task to be completed successfully. When the task is accomplished, Alexa responds with the message: "The reminder was successfully set." If a reminder was set and the time to has come, the speaker automatically activates and announces: "It is time to start your therapy! Launch the skill and say, 'I am at home'."

Starting Therapy. The user can start the therapy session by saying "I am at home", even without a reminder, after which the voice assistant tells him/her to go into the previously defined room, saying "Go to $< RoomSetByCaregiver >$! If you are already there, tell me 'I am here!'"

4   Scenario

This section aims to describe a typical scenario in which the interaction paradigm in question is used. Taking into account the common structure of a home, in which multiple smart assistants are set and installed, the following tasks are performed. Patients are encouraged to do their daily exercises. It is worth mentioning that the role of a smart assistant is not just to provide practical and concrete guidance to the patient, but rather a way to engage and keep him motivated. The exercises performed by the child are tracked, recorded and available for the monitoring of the speech therapist and the caregiver [9].

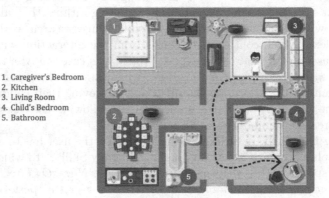

1. Caregiver's Bedroom
2. Kitchen
3. Living Room
4. Child's Bedroom
5. Bathroom

Fig. 2. Smart Home example

Figure 2 shows how the child interacts with the smart assistant following the instructions given. As previously mentioned, at the right time, Alexa wakes up and enunciates the following phrase *"It is time to start the therapy! Go to the $< RoomSetByCaregiver >$. If you are already there, tell me 'I am here'!"*. The assistant then says *"Let us start!"* and launches e-SpeechT on a device that was set by the caregiver in the configuration phase. The union between the web application and the smart assistant has the goal of reinforcing the patient's autonomy while preserving the medical feasibility of speech therapy.

5   Conclusions and Future Works

E-health is a field that is spreading and evolving at a very fast pace. Including AI techniques and sophisticated algorithms can bring numerous advantages to the world of medicine, such as the possibility for patients to perform treatments remotely in a familiar environment and for therapists to monitor their progress in therapy even long distances. In this study, these concepts are considered in the field of speech therapy with the aim of allowing children to perform the assigned exercises at home and consequently to ensure that the task is not perceived as boring or compulsory, but rather as a fun and enjoyable activity. In fact, the goal is to evoke feelings of excitement and curiosity in children. This aspect is enhanced due to the interaction between the children and the smart assistant Alexa, which allows patients to feel less under examination and away from the seriousness of the medical world. In conclusion, this research work aims to find a solution to empower people and support them in performing time-consuming and difficult tasks. The future work of this research encompasses the enhancement and automation of the amalgamation between e-SpeechT and Amazon Alexa. More specifically, the current state of the implemented skill involves a localization feature, which is currently in its preliminary stages. This feature aims to facilitate the voice assistant in determining whether the child is actually at home or not. Furthermore, an addition to this feature might involve the exploration of speech recognition techniques to enable voice authentication for the child on the e-SpeechT. The APIs offered by Amazon are not accurate and precise enough [3]. Consequently, this voice authentication feature will require external APIs and specific algorithms outside of the Alexa-hosted skill environment. In fact, it is planned to create an alternative version of this Amazon Alexa skill beyond the confines of the Amazon Development framework, thereby gaining access to a broader array of functionalities and features with the aim of increasing the medical feasibility and the ease of use of the whole interaction paradigm. It is also intended to improve e-SpeechT when it comes to providing a patient-specific learning process, reinforcing the concept of adaptive learning; the latter would result in a better learning experience for children by making it less stressful, more effective and less expensive time wise [17]. To ultimately determine the medical feasibility of this research work and to understand its strengths, weaknesses, and challenges a user study is necessary, in which all actors would be involved and the interaction paradigm can be tested in its entirety.

References

1. Speech-Language Pathologists: About Speech-Language Pathology (1990). https://www.asha.org/students/speech-language-pathologists
2. Speech and language therapy interventions for children with primary speech and/or language disorders (2017)
3. Amazon: Amazon Developer Documentation. https://developer.amazon.com/en-US/docs/alexa/custom-skills/add-personalization-to-your-skill.html
4. Barletta, V.S., Caivano, D., Colizzi, L., Dimauro, G., Piattini, M.: Clinical-chatbot AHP evaluation based on "quality in use" of ISO/IEC 25010. Int. J. Med. Informatics **170**, 104951 (2023). https://doi.org/10.1016/j.ijmedinf.2022.104951
5. Barletta, V.S., Caruso, F., Di Mascio, T., Piccinno, A.: Serious games for autism based on immersive virtual reality: a lens on methodological and technological challenges. In: Temperini, M., et al. (eds.) Methodologies and Intelligent Systems for Technology Enhanced Learning, 12th International Conference, pp. 181–195. Springer, Cham (2023). https://doi.org/10.1007/978-3-031-20617-7_23
6. Barletta, V.S., Cassano, F., Marengo, A., Pagano, A., Pange, J., Piccinno, A.: Switching learning methods during the pandemic: a quasi-experimental study on a master course. Appl. Sci. **12**(17) (2022). https://doi.org/10.3390/app12178438

7. Barletta, V.S., Cassano, F., Pagano, A., Piccinno, A.: A collaborative AI dataset creation for speech therapies. In: CEUR Workshop Proceedings, vol. 3136, pp. 81–85. CEUR-WS (2022)
8. Cassano, F., Pagano, A., Piccinno, A.: Supporting speech therapies at (smart) home through voice assistance. In: Novais, P., Carneiro, J., Chamoso, P. (eds.) Ambient Intelligence – Software and Applications – 12th International Symposium on Ambient Intelligence, pp. 105–113. Springer, Cham (2022). https://doi.org/10.1007/978-3-031-06894-2_10
9. Cassano, F., Piccinno, A., Regina, P.: End-user development in speech therapies: a scenario in the smart home domain. In: Malizia, A., Valtolina, S., Morch, A., Serrano, A., Stratton, A. (eds.) IS-EUD 2019. LNCS, vol. 11553, pp. 158–165. Springer, Cham (2019). https://doi.org/10.1007/978-3-030-24781-2_11
10. Huang, R.X., Pagano, A., Marengo, A.: Building a pedagogical framework for the education of sustainable development using a values-based education approach. In: 2021 Third International Sustainability and Resilience Conference: Climate Change, pp. 78–82 (2021)
11. Jothi, K.R., Sivaraju, S.S., Yawalkar, P.J.: AI based speech language therapy using speech quality parameters for aphasia person: a comprehensive review. In: 2020 4th International Conference on Electronics, Communication and Aerospace Technology (ICECA), pp. 1263–1271 (2020)
12. Kalmpourtzis, G.: Educational Game Design Fundamentals: A Journey to Creating Intrinsically Motivating Learning Experiences, 1st edn, p. 72. Taylor & Francis Group (2019)
13. Laws, G., Bishop, D.V.: A comparison of language abilities in adolescents with down syndrome and children with specific language impairment (2003)
14. Marengo, A., et al.: Game-based learning in mobile technology. In: 17th International Conference on Intelligent Games on Simulation, GAME-ON, pp. 80–84 (2016)
15. Mekebayev, N., Mamyrbayev, O.J., Turdalyuly, M., Oralbekova, D., Tasbolatov, M.: Algorithms and architectures of speech recognition systems (2021)
16. Murero, M., Vita, S., Mennitto, A., D'Ancona, G.: Artificial intelligence for severe speech impairment: innovative approaches to AAC and communication. In: PSYCHOBIT (2020)
17. Pagano, A., Marengo, A.: Training time optimization through adaptive learning strategy. In: 2021 International Conference on Innovation and Intelligence for Informatics, Computing, and Technologies (3ICT), pp. 563–567 (2021)
18. Schipor, O., Pentiuc, S., Schipor, M.: The utilization of feedback and emotion recognition in computer based speech therapy system. Elektronika ir Elektrotechnika 109(3), 101–104 (2011)
19. Wynn, R., Gabarron, E., Johnsen, J.A.K., Traver, V.: Special issue on e-health services. Int. J. Environ. Res. Publ. Health 17(8) (2020)
20. Xu, Y., et al.: Artificial intelligence: a powerful paradigm for scientific research. The Innovation 2(4), 100179 (2021)
21. Yujian, L., Bo, L.: A normalized Levenshtein distance metric. IEEE Trans. Pattern Anal. Mach. Intell. 29(6), 1091–1095 (2007)

2nd Workshop on Engineering Processes and Practices for Quantum Software (PPQS'23)

Integration of Classical and Quantum Services Using an Enterprise Service Bus

Javier Bonilla[1]([📧])(ⓘ), Enrique Moguel[2](ⓘ), José García-Alonso[2](ⓘ),
and Carlos Canal[1](ⓘ)

[1] University of Málaga, ITIS Software, Málaga, Spain
{jbonillac,carloscanal}@uma.es
[2] University of Extremadura, Escuela Politécnica,
Quercus Software Engineering Group, Cáceres, Spain
{enrique,jgaralo}@unex.es

Abstract. Early advancements in quantum computing have opened up new possibilities to tackle complex problems across various fields, including mathematics, physics, and healthcare. However, the technology required to construct systems where different quantum and classical software components collaborate is currently lacking. To address this, substantial progress in service-oriented quantum computing is necessary, empowering developers to create and operate quantum services and microservices that are comparable to their classical counterparts. The main objective of this work is to establish the essential technological infrastructure for integrating an Enterprise Service Bus (ESB). This integration enables developers to implement quantum algorithms through independent and automatable services, thereby facilitating the collaboration of quantum and classical software components. Additionally, this work has been validated through a practical case using Zato, a platform that supports service-oriented architectures. By achieving this goal, developers can harness the power of quantum computing while benefiting from the flexibility, scalability, and efficiency of service-oriented computing. This integration opens up new possibilities for developing advanced quantum applications and tackling real-world challenges across various domains.

Keywords: Quantum Computing · Enterprise Service Bus · ESB · Hybrid Quantum Computation · Service Integration

1 Introduction

Quantum computing is already a reality [13]. It offers great possibilities to accelerate calculations or create entirely new algorithms. This is achieved thanks to the properties that quantum physics provides us, such as superposition and entanglement [8]. Through the power of quantum physics, quantum computing can accelerate algorithms that have extremely long run times or sub-optimal results in classical computers. It even can execute completely new algorithms that can expose new and faster ways to find results, such as Shor's algorithm

R. Kadgien et al. (Eds.): PROFES 2023, LNCS 14484, pp. 107–118, 2024.
https://doi.org/10.1007/978-3-031-49269-3_11

with the factorization of integers [17]. The fields that can now use quantum computing are as diverse as machine learning [6], physical and chemical simulation [3], and optimization algorithms [14].

But despite its potential benefits, the current state of the art for programming quantum algorithms is still in its infancy. Most quantum programming frameworks only offer the implementation of algorithms at a very low-level approach, through circuits, and must be written in monolithic scripts. That also collides with the fact that the most valuable quantum algorithms are not pure quantum processes. These algorithms are what is called *Hybrid quantum-classical algorithms*, such as the Quantum Approximate Optimization Algorithm (QAOA) [7] or the Variational Quantum Eigensolver (VQE) [16].

The main problem with the current quantum programming frameworks, like *Qiskit*[1], *Amazon Braket SDK*[2] or *Cirq*[3] is that the solution they provide is writing that algorithm in the same script. The problem with this approach is the fact that the programmer performs very low-level repetitive tasks, such as the configuration of the quantum computer where the script is to be executed. While the developer performs all these repetitive tasks, the developer can lose focus on what he wants to do with that algorithm or the integration of that algorithm with a more complex system (see Sect. 2).

There are also other limitations to this approach. For example, the execution of the classical section must be run on the same machine where the script is located and that part may require considerable computation resources. Another problem is that the classical part can be executed in parallel or doesn't need to wait until the quantum part is completed. In this context, with the current approach, that cannot be done easily because the script is run in the same thread.

To address these problems, in this paper, we present our approach to create and integrate quantum and classical services using an Enterprise Service Bus (ESB), namely Zato[4], an open-source Python ESB. The architecture of Zato allows the implementation of quantum algorithms through independent and automatable services. This approach offers to step up in the abstraction layer, letting the developer focus on the important things and leaving the repetitive task to Zato. It also makes easier the integration of quantum algorithms into classical workflows using current modelling languages, such as the Business Process Model and Notation (BPMN), with the modifications required to take into account the particularities of quantum computing.

In summary, this proposal allows the creation of quantum services that can be integrated into classical workflow models using the ESB architectural pattern. Moreover, this approach allows eliminating all repetitive configurations of the algorithm execution, thus simplifying the developers' work.

The rest of the paper has the following structure. Section 2 analyzes the motivation of the present work. Section 3 presents the proposed solution to create quantum services integrated into classical workflows. To expose it, it is intro-

---

[1] https://qiskit.org/.
[2] https://github.com/aws/amazon-braket-sdk-python.
[3] https://quantumai.google/cirq.
[4] https://zato.io/.

duced a brief explanation of Zato and the BPMN, then the proper extension, and finally a basic BPMN to Zato parser. Section 4 features a case study to justify the usefulness of the proposal of this work. Section 5 relates the state of the art to the work done.

2 Research Context and Motivation

The vast majority of quantum programming frameworks use scripts to define quantum tasks. These scripts specify everything necessary for the execution of the task. They include the definition of the circuit; the processing of the input and output data, if necessary; the classical computing parts, if the program is a hybrid quantum algorithm; and the selection and configuration of the quantum computer or simulator where that code is going to be executed.

In Fig. 1 we find a script representing a circuit that implements a Bell state [18] and executes it on an AWS quantum simulator. However, only one line (line 8) refers to the quantum circuit itself. Apart from importing Amazon's Boto and Braket frameworks, the rest of the script deals with the configuration and execution of the circuit in the simulator (specified in line 19), and with showing the results (line 24). Thus, the vast majority of the code that defines a quantum task has nothing to do with the proper representation of the circuit itself, but with instructions for its execution in a particular platform, and other issues not directly related to the quantum algorithm being executed.

```
1 import boto3
2
3 from braket.aws import AwsDevice
4 from braket.devices import LocalSimulator
5 from braket.circuits import Circuit
6
7 # create the circuit
8 bell = Circuit().h(0).cnot(0, 1)
9
10 # get the account ID
11 aws_account_id = boto3.client("sts").get_caller_identity()["Account"]
12 # the name of the bucket
13 my_bucket = "amazon-braket-prueba-tareas"
14 # the name of the folder in the bucket
15 my_prefix = "tareas"
16 s3_folder = (my_bucket, my_prefix)
17
18 # choose the cloud-based on-demand simulator to run your circuit
19 device = AwsDevice("arn:aws:braket:::device/quantum-simulator/amazon/sv1")
20
21 # execute the circuit
22 task = device.run(bell, s3_folder, shots=100)
23 # display the results
24 print(task.result().measurement_counts)
```

Fig. 1. Python script of a circuit implementing the Bell state using AWS Braket

If we look at more complex scenarios, this problem is exacerbated. Apart from the repetitive part of the configuration and execution of the algorithm in the quantum computer, the quantum task often includes classical pre or post-processing that has nothing to do with the quantum code. Moreover, the tasks need to deal with waiting for the results with execution times that can be extremely long in currently available quantum machines.

The problems mentioned above can be addressed using classical Software Engineering techniques, such as service integration [12]. These techniques facilitate the definition of hybrid quantum algorithms by conceptually splitting the algorithm into different services. Moreover, the integration of quantum algorithms into existing classical workflows would be much easier. Additionally, the introduction of synchronization logic either between task components or within the entire workflow would be automated.

For these reasons, we have explored the possibility of extending existing tools in the field of classical computing —in particular Zato— that allow us to define complex tasks and workflows. The focus of this paper is to create services that help run quantum programs focusing on the definition of the quantum circuit, and how it is integrated in classical computing workflow.

3   Integration of Quantum Services into Existing Workflow and ESB Tools

In this section we will present our proposal, introducing first a short description of Zato and its benefits, and the BPMN modelling language. After that, we present how to extend them for quantum processes. Finally, we explain the development of a simple translator from BPMN to Zato.

3.1   Business Process Model and Notation

BPMN is a standard developed by the Object Management Group (OMG) to provide a common notation to define business processes that are understandable by all business users. BPMN is a large standard that can be used in numerous scenarios and use cases. In this section, we describe the basic elements composing a BPMN diagram.

BPMN is composed of diagrams that contain at least the following basic elements: 1) **Events** which represent something that happens during a process and affect the flow of the model. There are three types of Events: Start, Intermediate, and End Events; 2) **Activities** which represent the work that a company performs; 3) **Gateways** which are responsible for the synchronization of flows in the model. There are many types of gateways, but the two most important are the exclusive and parallel gateway; and 4) **Sequence Flows** which represent the order in which the Activities will be performed.

These basic elements allow us to build a diagram to represent any business process. However, BPMN does not take into account the particularities of quantum tasks. For example, the different attributes necessary for executing a quantum algorithm or the quantum provider in which the algorithm will be executed. To address these issues, we provide a basic BPMN to the Zato translator, taking into account these problems (see Sect. 3.4).

3.2   Zato: Description and Benefits

Zato is a widely used open-source Python platform that allows to build and deliver enterprise solutions, from online APIs, business processes, data science, AI, IoT, mainframe and cloud migrations, etc., combining ease of use with safety and security. Zato is developed as a highly distributed system with various Zato instances, which are called *clusters*. The main benefits of using Zato are:

- It scales horizontally in a potential environment of thousands of services with minimal system overhead.
- Each cluster may run in different geographical locations, or on different servers. Each cluster contains a Zato environment with a load balancer, a scheduler, a web-based dashboard for administration, and one or more servers where the services execute.
- Zato allows *hot-deployment*. Whenever a new version of a service is deployed on a server, all other servers will synchronize that information, and only that one service will be reconfigured and changed with no need to restart the rest of them. This functionality allows services to be exchanged quickly, in the order of milliseconds, without stopping the whole system.
- Zatos uses Python for all service definitions and synchronization. This is also useful because the overwhelming majority of quantum programming frameworks are done in Python and this facilitates the integration of implementing quantum services into Zato.

For these and other benefits, such as the implementation of Zato is open source, and we have chosen this tool to present our proposal for integrating quantum services in general software workflows.

3.3   Extending of Zato for Supporting Quantum Services

The first thing we had to address was how to introduce quantum services within the existing Zato architecture. In Zato, all services, whether user-created or system-created, inherit from a Python base class called `Service`, which contains all the methods and functionality that a service requires.

Thus, we created a new `QuantumService` class that extends the base class `Service`. This class inherits all the functionality that a classical service has, but the philosophy of classical Zato services is completely changed. In a classic Zato service, the only part that Zato itself executes is the method `handle`. The service may have other auxiliary methods, but in the end, all synchronization and execution logic must be done or called in the `handle` function.

However, this approach cannot be used in a quantum service, which needs to be run on a quantum computer. Quantum services need to specify additional parameters: the quantum computer where we want the code to be run, the number of runs of the algorithm, or the threshold that is required for that service to be considered a reliable execution. These attributes can be specified in the quantum service class either as class attributes or as function parameters when we call the quantum service from another service by using Zato's methods `invoke` or `invoke_async`, for synchronous and asynchronous invocation, respectively.

The solution that we came up with is to define two required methods that must be implemented in the quantum service, as shown in Fig. 2. First, the `circuit` method, in which the circuit is defined, and then the `after_circuit_execution` method with an attribute for the result of the execution, where we can implement the logic after the circuit execution and the post-processing of the result. There is the additional `before_circuit_execution` method, in which we can implement pre-processing, i.e. logic before the circuit executes.

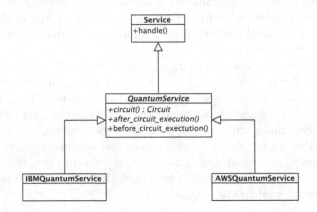

Fig. 2. Basic class diagram of the extension implemented

An important clarification before continuing is the fact that in this paper we have used the general UML profile, instead of specific profiles for quantum systems as proposed in [15]. The `QuantumService` class is an abstract class, as it does not implement itself where the quantum code will be run. This is delegated to the children's classes that define which provider will be used, as seen in Fig. 2. Thus, our approach can be easily extended by creating additional subclasses of `QuantumService`. At the moment, we offer the possibility to specify and execute services for the IBM Quantum and Amazon Braket services, through the `IBMQuantumService` and `AWSQuantumService` classes, respectively.

The `QuantumService` class is not a mere wrapper for executing quantum circuits. It is also responsible for synchronizing the pre- and post-processing of the result. It also checks if the code reaches the threshold defined, and it allows it to specify if the code needs to be repeated if it does not reach that threshold. Its subclasses are also responsible for configuring and executing the quantum circuit, using the attributes of the service: number of runs, timeout, or the computer where the code will be run. Finally, it also gets the keys necessary for authenticating into the cloud providers using the Zato built-in key database.

While implementing this extension, we came up with an important limitation of Zato. It does not offer any configuration mechanism for the synchronization of services. All service synchronization and integration must be coded in Python in the service definition itself. Therefore, we decided to extend BPMN for using it for a workflow definition of the whole quantum task, and we implemented a translator of a basic subset of BPMN into our Zato quantum services. This will be explained in the next subsection.

3.4   BPMN to Zato Translator

As mentioned above, in Zato, all of the configuration and synchronization of services is done in the definition of the services itself. This makes implementing hybrid classical/quantum workflows into Zato a manual and tedious task. It is also prone to errors when the workflow has a non-trivial size and complexity.

For this reason, we considered it appropriate to create a small translator from BPMN to Zato. This translator would at least take into account a basic subset of BPMN, to help in the creation of services. Obviously, in the translator we took into account the new quantum services and all their specific configuration properties.

Definition of   XML file specifing   BPMN to   Zato
BPMN Diagram   the BPMN diagram   Zato parser   services

Fig. 3. High-level diagram representing the flow for translating a BPMN diagram into Zato services

As seen in Fig. 3, showing the workflow for using the translator, we first define the BPMN diagram and export it into an XML file. Then, this XML file is introduced into the parser and outputs the Zato services that implement the BPMN workflow. The generated services can be immediately deployed in Zato.

To differentiate between classic and quantum services, we have used BPMN stereotypes. For quantum services, the activity is assigned the *Quantum Task* stereotype. If the translator finds this stereotype, it creates a quantum service that inherits from `QuantumService`, instead of a classical Zato service.

```
{
    "provider": "ibm",
    "quantum_computer": "ibmq_qasm_simulator",
    "runs": "1000",
    "threshold": "0.5"
}
```

Fig. 4. Example of the configuration attributes for quantum services

The quantum services also need the definition of their specific attributes. To address it, we specify these attributes in the description of the service specification in BPMN diagram tools. There, it is represented by a JSON document, as seen in Fig. 4, where the quantum service properties previously described are specified. When the parser identifies these attributes, if it reads "ibm", the services will inherit from IBMQuantumService, and if it reads "aws" or "amazon", will inherit from AWSQuantumService. In case of failure, the parser will inherit the generic QuantumService class.

In the following section, we will go in-depth into the features of our extension to BPMN and Zato through a case study.

4   Case Study: Implementing QAOA with Zato Quantum Services

To show the full potential of the proposal introduced in this paper, we present a case study where we transform a script implementing QAOA into a series of Zato services that will get the same results.

The Quantum Approximate Optimization Algorithm (QAOA) is a hybrid quantum-classical variational algorithm designed to tackle combinatorial optimization problems [21]. In this algorithm, a quantum computer prepares a quantum state using parametrized values. After measuring the output, these parameters are optimized in a classical optimization algorithm and then feedback again in the quantum computer in a closed loop.

The input of the QAOA is a Hamiltonian that encodes the objective function that we want to be optimized. The problems that can take advantage of QAOA are the Knapsack problem [11], the MaxCut problem [4], or the Traveling Salesman problem [10].

The script that will be used as starting point is provided by Amazon AWS, and it can be found in the repository[5]. Also, the resulting Zato services can be found in this repository[6]

The script is of considerable length (170 lines of code) and it mixes in different functions: the definition of the quantum circuit that implements QAOA with the classical contains a section that obtains the costs by interpreting the output of the quantum circuit.

The first step is to find where the script can be broken into the quantum and classical parts for creating a classic service and a quantum service. This is easy because the script is divided into numerous functions and each one is dedicated to the different functionalities required for the algorithm. For example, there is a function for running the circuit in the specified computer passed by reference and the different attributes necessary or different circuit subroutines

---

[5] https://github.com/aws-samples/amazon-braket-algorithm-library/blob/main/src/braket/experimental/algorithms/quantum_approximate_optimization/quantum_approximate_optimization.py.

[6] https://github.com/javibc3/qaoa-zato-services.

for implementing the different layers and gates necessary for the circuit (see all the functions that have the @circuit.subroutine(register=True) decorator).

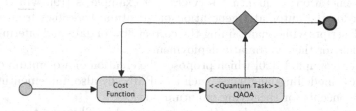

Fig. 5. BPMN diagram representing the services implementing QAOA

Based on this, the script has been divided into two services, a quantum service called qaoa, which is in charge of all the definition and configuration of the quantum part, and a classical service, called qaoaCostFunction, which implements the preprocessing, the interpretation of the quantum execution result and the execution of the classical optimization algorithm using the quantum results (see Fig. 5).

Our approach helps integrate the algorithm with its inputs and outputs. For example, we can connect the input matrix with a service that implements a quantum random number generator (QRNG) (see the qaoaQrngInput.py service in the Zato service repository). A QRNG is a random number generator (RNG) that instead of using mathematical functions or predefined tables employs properties of quantum physics, such as superposition to generate the numbers.

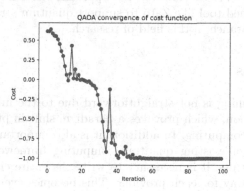

Fig. 6. Convergence graph of the QAOA cost function

We can also connect the output to produce a graph with the cost descent (see Fig. 6) which is sent by mail or displayed on the system where Zato is running (see the qaoaOutputMail.py, qaoaShowImage.py and qaoaCreateImage.py services in the Zato service repository).

5   Related Work

Even though it is a new field of research, there are already several works dealing with the generation of quantum services. An example is [19], which proposes a solution for the automatic generation of quantum workflows from quantum framework scripts while maintaining the correct flow of data and offering deployment models for their automatic deployment.

Another example is [20] which proposes the creation of a quantum extension for workflow modelling languages, such as BPMN, by also implementing all the necessary concepts for specifying quantum services.

There are also works such as the one presented in [2] where the authors set out to mitigate read errors using quantum workflow models, automating these usually manual and cumbersome processes.

We can also look into the field of *Quantum Computing as a Service* (QCaaS). Garcia-Alonso *et al.* [9] presents an implementation of the Quantum API Gateway pattern. This new pattern is an adaptation of the classical API Gateway that takes into account the conceptual differences between classic and quantum services. Ahmad *et al.* [1] also proposes an extensive reference architecture of *Quantum Computing as a Service* (QCaaS). In this paper, they expose an architecture that can build an entire quantum ecosystem around the as-a-service (aaS) concept and evaluate it between various practitioners. Lastly, De Stefano *et al.* [5] show us a roadmap to achieve *Quantum Algorithms as a Serivce* (QAaaS) model. This model offers the quantum algorithms as services, in which the users invoke them through API invocation, ignoring the technical specification below.

These works and some others that have been found in the literature focus on creating extensions to existing modelling languages or the automatic generation of generic quantum services. However, our approach starts from the extension of an already established tool like Zato to support quantum services, which is not a widely explored branch in this field of research.

6   Conclusions

Quantum programming is not straightforward due to the inherent difficulty of quantum computation, which provokes a paradigm shift in programmers accustomed to classical computing. In addition, it is also important to consider that the vast majority of existing quantum computing frameworks operate using scripts. In these scripts, it is necessary to write the entire circuit specification, and in a different way for each provider. This becomes even more challenging when implementing hybrid quantum algorithms, as they involve the combination of quantum and classical modules. The classical script-based approach induces a monolithic implementation in a single script, which greatly limits scalability and the integration of these algorithms with other classical services.

For these reasons, we have presented in this paper an extension of zato, an established and widely used tool that implements the ESB architecture pattern to create quantum services that can be integrated into classical workflow models.

We have created quantum services taking into account the specific parameters necessary for the correct operation of the quantum modules. Also, our approach allows for removing all the repetitive configurations of the execution of the algorithm and focuses only on the definition of the quantum circuit itself. It also allows scaling and reutilizing implemented algorithms into different workflows, using components that can be interchanged with little rewriting. Our proposal allows quantum computing to increase its usefulness in the real world. The integration of quantum services opens up a wide range of possibilities to improve established processes. It also allows to establishment of new hybrid processes, which help to speed up many computing tasks.

As future work, we plan to support additional providers such as Azure or Google Cloud, to name a few. Our proposal may also be extended to support parameters that were not contemplated in this work. In addition, the BPMN to Zato parser may be extended to take into account BPMN extensions as in [20].

Acknowledgment. This work has been partially funded by MCIN/AEI/10.13039/501100011033 and by the EU "Next GenerationEU/PRTR", by the Ministry of Science, Innovation and Universities (projects PID2021-124045OB-C31, TED2021-130913B-I00, PDC2022-133465-I00). It is also supported by the QSALUD project (EXP 00135977/MIG-20201059) in the lines of action of the CDTI; by the Ministry of Economic Affairs and Digital Transformation of the Spanish Government through the Quantum ENIA project - Quantum Spain project; by the EU through the Recovery, Transformation, and Resilience Plan - NextGenerationEU within the framework of the Digital Spain 2025 Agenda; and by the Regional Ministry of Economy, Science and Digital Agenda (GR21133).

References

1. Ahmad, A., Altamimi, A.B., Aqib, J.: A reference architecture for quantum computing as a service (2023)
2. Beisel, M., Barzen, J., Leymann, F., Truger, F., Weder, B., Yussupov, V.: Configurable readout error mitigation in quantum workflows. Electronics **11**(19) (2022). https://doi.org/10.3390/electronics11192983
3. Cao, Y., et al.: Quantum chemistry in the age of quantum computing. Chem. Rev. **119**, 10856–10915 (2019). https://doi.org/10.1021/ACS.CHEMREV.8B00803
4. Commander, C.: Maximum cut problem, MAX-CUT . In: Floudas, C., Pardalos, P. (eds.) Encyclopedia of Optimization. Springer, Boston, MA, pp. 1991–1999 (2008). https://doi.org/10.1007/978-0-387-74759-0_358
5. De Stefano, M., Di Nucci, D., Palomba, F., Taibi, D., De Lucia, A.: Towards quantum-algorithms-as-a-service. In: Proceedings of the 1st International Workshop on Quantum Programming for Software Engineering, QP4SE 2022, pp. 7–10. Association for Computing Machinery, New York, NY, USA (2022). https://doi.org/10.1145/3549036.3562056
6. Dunjko, V., Briegel, H.J.: Machine learning & artificial intelligence in the quantum domain: a review of recent progress. Rep. Prog. Phys. **81**, 074001 (2018). https://doi.org/10.1088/1361-6633/AAB406
7. Farhi, E., Goldstone, J., Gutmann, S.: A quantum approximate optimization algorithm. arXiv arXiv1411.4028 (2014)

8. Forcer, T.M., Hey, A.J., Ross, D., Smith, P.: Superposition, entanglement and quantum computation. Quantum Inf. Comput. **2**(2), 97–116 (2002)
9. Garcia-Alonso, J., Rojo, J., Valencia, D., Moguel, E., Berrocal, J., Murillo, J.M.: Quantum software as a service through a quantum API gateway. IEEE Internet Comput. **26**(1), 34–41 (2022). https://doi.org/10.1109/MIC.2021.3132688
10. Hoffman, K.L., Padberg, M.: Traveling salesman problem (TSP) traveling salesman problem, pp. 849–853. Springer, US, New York, NY (2001). https://doi.org/10.1007/1-4020-0611-X_1068
11. Korte, B., Vygen, J.: The knapsack problem. In: Combinatorial Optimization. Algorithms and Combinatorics, vol. 21, pp. 397–406. Springer, Berlin (2002). https://doi.org/10.1007/978-3-662-21711-5_17
12. Moguel, E., Rojo, J., Valencia, D., Berrocal, J., Garcia-Alonso, J., Murillo, J.M.: Quantum service-oriented computing: current landscape and challenges. Software Qual. J. **30**, 983–1002 (2022). https://doi.org/10.1007/S11219-022-09589-Y
13. Mohan, B., Das, S., Pati, A.K., Gholizadeh, A., Hadipour, M., Haseli, S.: Quantum speed limits: from heisenberg's uncertainty principle to optimal quantum control. J. Phys. A: Math. Theor. **50**, 453001 (2017). https://doi.org/10.1088/1751-8121/AA86C6
14. Moll, N., et al.: Quantum optimization using variational algorithms on near-term quantum devices. Quantum Sci. Technol. **3**(3), 030503 (2018). https://doi.org/10.1088/2058-9565/aab822
15. Pérez-Castillo, R., Piattini, M.: Design of classical-quantum systems with UML. Computing **104**(11), 2375–2403 (2022). https://doi.org/10.1007/s00607-022-01091-4
16. Peruzzo, A., et al.: A variational eigenvalue solver on a photonic quantum processor. Nat. Commun. **5**(1) (2014). https://doi.org/10.1038/ncomms5213
17. Shor, P.W.: Polynomial-time algorithms for prime factorization and discrete logarithms on a quantum computer. SIAM J. Comput. **26**(5), 1484–1509 (1997). https://doi.org/10.1137/s0097539795293172
18. Sych, D., Leuchs, G.: A complete basis of generalized bell states. New J. Phys. **11**(1), 013006 (2009). https://doi.org/10.1088/1367-2630/11/1/013006
19. Vietz, D., Barzen, J., Leymann, F., Weder, B.: Splitting quantum-classical scripts for the generation of quantum workflows. In: Almeida, J.P.A., Karastoyanova, D., Guizzardi, G., Montali, M., Maggi, F.M., Fonseca, C.M. (eds.) Enterprise Design, Operations, and Computing. EDOC 2022. LNCS, vol. 13585, pp 255–270. Springer, Cham (2022). https://doi.org/10.1007/978-3-031-17604-3_15
20. Weder, B., Breitenbücher, U., Leymann, F., Wild, K.: Integrating quantum computing into workflow modeling and execution. In: 2020 IEEE/ACM 13th International Conference on Utility and Cloud Computing (UCC), pp. 279–291 (2020). https://doi.org/10.1109/UCC48980.2020.00046
21. Zhou, L., Wang, S.T., Choi, S., Pichler, H., Lukin, M.D.: Quantum approximate optimization algorithm: performance, mechanism, and implementation on near-term devices. Phys. Rev. X **10**(2) (2020). https://doi.org/10.1103/physrevx.10.021067

Problem Decomposition to Leverage Quantum Computing for Optimization Problems

Niraj Dayama(✉), Majid Haghparast, and Vlad Stirbu

University of Jyväskylä, Jyväskylä, Finland
{niraj.r.dayama,majid.m.haghparast,vlad.a.stirbu}@jyu.fi

Abstract. The emerging paradigm of Quantum computing has the potential to transform the established way-of-working in several scientific and industrial fields if the open challenges of applying quantum computing systems for real-world applications are addressed. One of the major challenges is that the quantum computing systems accessible for industrial and commercial users have very few qubits. Several research initiatives are being proposed to work around this constraint. We investigate the amenable scope and limits of a hybrid platform where classical computing works in tandem with quantum computing to address practical problems. Instead of focusing on quantum supremacy or specialized academic problems, this paper proposes a framework where generalized industrial applications can be solved using hybrid computing systems with limited qubit capacity using a decomposition technique that can be modified to any decision-support procedure.

Keywords: quantum computing · hybrid classical-quantum computing · branch-and-bound · tree-search algorithms · quantum optimization techniques

1 Introduction

The potential of quantum computing is being tapped to address problems in a plethora of topics. However, the practice of quantum computing is still in its infancy and faces several limitations. Three major challenges are: (1) build and maintain large-scale reliable and accurate quantum computers, (2) develop efficient and scalable quantum algorithms that can address practical problems [1] provably faster or better than classical algorithms, and (3) identify and quantify the quantum advantage or benefits gained by using quantum computers over classical computers for a given class of problems. Currently, there exist few examples of quantum computing applications where a clear quantum advantage has been proven while solving practical problems [2].

We consider that classical computing and quantum computing can co-exist and collaborate within a joint infrastructure setup (whether on the same physical system or via a cloud based system). A hybrid system consists of a classical

R. Kadgien et al. (Eds.): PROFES 2023, LNCS 14484, pp. 119–124, 2024.
https://doi.org/10.1007/978-3-031-49269-3_12

computer and a quantum co-processor connected by a feedback loop. Classical systems can perform reliable, fast, and scalable tasks such as data processing, error correction, and optimization. Quantum co-processor can handle tasks that are intractable for classical computers, such as factoring large numbers, and solving NP-hard problems. The feedback loop allows the classical computer to control the quantum co-processor based on the results of the measurements. The hybrid system can thus leverage the advantages of both classical and quantum systems while mitigating their limitations.

We propose to use a similar hybrid computing approach; But we will embed the quantum computing capability within an overall dynamic programming structure. Contrary to established practices of proving quantum supremacy, we will try to build a flexible algorithm that adapts itself to the available quantum capacity while relying on classical computing for the remaining computations. We assume that a generic mathematical decision-making problem $\mathbb{P}$ is to be solved. To solve this problem, a classical computational system $\mathbb{C}$ and also a quantum computational system $\mathbb{Q}$ is available. The quantum computing capability $\mathbb{Q}$ is restricted to q qubits only.

2   Background of Hybrid Computing Systems

Hybrid computational systems have been studied almost immediately along with the development of quantum computational facilities. The measurement-based variational quantum eigensolver (MB-VQE) algorithm discussed in [3] finds applications across chemistry, physics, and machine learning. Hybrid computational systems have also been applied to dynamic programming, similar to the intention of this paper. For example, [4] discusses a quantum algorithm for finding paths in n-dimensional lattice graphs, which are generalizations of the Boolean hypercube graph. Conversely, dynamic programming has been applied to address quantum computational problems. For example, [5] applies dynamic programming to a special class of quantum error correction protocols called quantum repeater protocols. These are used to overcome the exponential attenuation of quantum signals in noisy channels such as optical fibers. The paper finds significant improvements in both the speed and the final-state fidelity for preparing long-distance entangled states, which are essential resources for quantum cryptography and information processing.

3   Decision Support Assisted by Quantum Computing

3.1   Textual Description of Decomposition Approach

Addressing $\mathbb{P}$ as a multi-step decision tree, we start traversing the branch-and-bound tree in a depth-first manner using the classical computational system $\mathbb{C}$ alone. Focusing on the deepest (final) leaf nodes during the initial classical computations, we determine the maximum number m of leaf node computations that can be performed within a single quantum circuit based on the available quantum computing capability $\mathbb{Q}$. Obviously, m is a function of q and also depends on

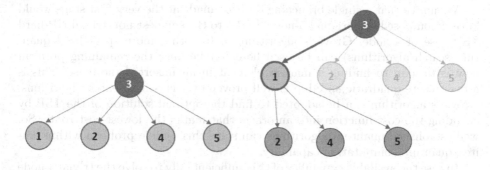

Fig. 1. Decomposition stages: every child node represents an independent NP-Hard problem (left); every child node represents a trivial problem with no further decisions required, only computation of total cost is required (right)

the problem $\mathbb{P}$. Existence of a stable m value also requires that the computation of the value of a state (or objective function of a candidate solution) should be possible within a fixed and known amount of computation effort. This is equivalent to the oracle of values for state spaces in classical dynamic programming context.

The value of m will be reliably known after traversing a few leaf nodes of the decision tree using classical computational system $\mathbb{C}$ alone. Now consider the traversal of these m leaf nodes as a specific stand-alone computational exercise. By design, the size of this computational task was defined such that the quantum computing capability $\mathbb{Q}$ can handle the required m nodes. So, the specific computational task can be delegated to the quantum computing capability $\mathbb{Q}$ while the overall branch-and-bound structure continues to be handled by the classical computational system $\mathbb{C}$. This ensures that the overall algorithm can flexibly match whatever quantum capability q is available while also getting the overall results handled by the classical computer.

3.2   Illustration of Decomposition Approach

We illustrate our approach using the classical case of the traveling salesman problem. Consider a TSP being solved for a 5-city (5-node) case with no special considerations or side constraints. The distance matrix D_{ij} specified the distance between the cities $\{1, 2, 3, 4, 5\}$.

Without loss of generality, we assume that our tour starts from city 3. Immediately after 3, the tour can visit any one of $\{1, 2, 4, 5\}$. So, we make a decision tree with four branches from 3. Since we traverse the decision tree in a depth-first approach, we select child node 1 for next exploration. Traversal of node 1 indicates that the tour segment $3 \rightarrow 1$ has been tentatively selected and the next node in the tour is now required. Here, the available options for further traversal are $\{2, 4, 5\}$. Those three nodes lead to the three potential decision branches from node 1 now. Further decomposition would involve the trivial 3-node TSP case and is not shown. The decomposition is illustrated in Fig. 1

We notice that a single branching decision made at the very first stage would have decomposed the original 5-node TSP into the smallest non-trivial NP-hard TSP case of 4-node. Grover's algorithm [6] (or other more specialized quantum search algorithms) can be used hereafter because the remaining problem now is to akin to finding a marked element in an unsorted database. This is a task where quadratic speedup is well proven over classical search algorithms. Grover's algorithm can be adapted to find the optimal solution of the TSP by encoding the cost function into an oracle that marks the lowest-cost route. So, well-established quantum algorithms can solve this 4-node problem within limited quantum computation capability.

In case the available capability of $\mathbb{Q}$ is sufficient only to solve the trivial 3-node TSP via an oracle lookup, we utilize $\mathbb{C}$ to execute the entire tree traversal upto the 3-node. That will result in a negligible improvement in overall performance and so the use of a hybrid computing capability may not be justified. In case the available capability of $\mathbb{Q}$ is sufficient to solve the non-trivial 4-node case, the resulting overall quantum speed-up may now justify the use of hybrid computing so that the quantum capability does lead to a noticeable speedup. In practice, we are now seeing 400+ qubit processors (example: IBM Osprey 433 qubits in November 2022) that provide sufficient qubits and gates to execute Gate-based quantum algorithms for large problem sizes.

The authors strongly acknowledge that - contrary to illustration above - exact solutions of TSP are not determined with an explicit enumeration of decision trees. The illustration was intended to explain our hybrid computing approach and was not intended as the dominant solution for TSP. Rather, we content that the same approach is required (and quite effective) for cases where implicit enumeration is not possible and when computation of objective values for potential solutions is a non-trivial non-linear task. Since this category covers a wide variety of decision-support problems, we expect our algorithm to find wide applicability.

Algorithm 1: Applicability of Decomposition Algorithm for specific decision-making problem

---

Data: $q \geq 0 \longleftrightarrow$ Number of qubits available
/* Initial pass: Compute m */
$S \leftarrow \mathbb{P}$ $depth \leftarrow 0$ **while** $||S|| \geq q$ **do**
$\quad | \quad S \leftarrow (>> S)$ $depth \leftarrow (depth + 1)$;
end
$m \leftarrow ||S||$; **Result:** $m, depth$ values

3.3   Algorithms for Decomposition Approach

Algorithm 1 intends to confirm or reject the applicability of our decomposition approach to any specific decision-making problem. It uses the notation $||.||$ to indicate the number of qubits required to completely solve a specific sub-problem in the absence of any separate classical computing capability. The notation $(>> S)$ indicates that the first decision required for solving sub-problem S

has been made randomly leading to a shorter sub-problem. The results $m, depth$ of Algorithm 1 help deduce whether quantum speed-up gained is worth the additional overheads of utilizing the quantum capability. Here traversal upto $depth$ will be required by classical computing $\mathbb{C}$. Thereafter, quantum computing will solve the remaining problem of size m. Summation of these computational efforts yields the total computation efforts in solving $\mathbb{P}$ using hybrid setup of $\mathbb{C}$ and $\mathbb{Q}$.

Next, we assume that the results $m, depth$ of Algorithm 1 are promising enough. Then we discuss the actual decomposition algorithm. This algorithm is generic enough to address a plethora of branch-and-bound decision schemes.

Algorithm 2: Decomposition to solve decision-making problem $\mathbb{P}$

Data: $m \geq 0 \longleftrightarrow$ Max size for $\mathbb{Q}$
Data: $\Theta \longleftrightarrow$ Initial feasible solution
$\Pi \leftarrow \{\mathbb{P}\}$ as top-level unsolved node **while** $|\Pi| \geq 0$ **do**
    $\theta \leftarrow NSA(\Pi)$
    if $Val(\theta) \leq Val(\Theta)$ and $Val(\Theta)$ *known* **then**
    | Exit WHILE loop
    end
    if *Problem size of* $\theta \leq m$ **then**
        Solve θ as a Quantum problem
        if $Val(\theta) \geq Val(\Theta)$ **then**
        | $\Theta \leftarrow \theta$
        end
    end
    $\Pi \leftarrow \Pi \cup ACN(\theta) \setminus \{\theta\}$
end
Result: Θ as final solution

Algorithm 2 delegates to Q the largest possible sub-problem that Q can handle. It assumes that the initial feasible solution Θ is already known. The notation NSA denotes a node selection algorithm, which selects the best (most promising) hitherto unexplored node. All child nodes induced by the branch decisions of any specific node are obtained by ACN function. Π is a sorted dictionary data structure where unexplored nodes are stored for future consumption. The objective value of any feasible solution θ is denoted by function $Val(\theta)$. For partially explored nodes, $Val(\theta)$ is the upper limit on the objective value for any feasible solution induced by that partially explored note.

The algorithm starts by seeding Π with the top level unsolved node (in branch-and-bound or dynamic programming context). It is designed for a reward/value maximization nature of $\mathbb{P}$. As long as the dictionary structure Π has unexplored nodes, the *while* loop picks the most promising node via NSA. At this point, implicit enumeration and branch cutting has been included, but is is not a necessary requirement for this algorithm. If the most promising unexplored node is still too large for the quantum computer, then the node is further decomposed. The resulting sub-nodes are added to Π for future exploration. The problem is still within the realm of classical computing and so the *while* loop traversal continues. However, if the expected problem size of the most promising unexplored node is already smaller than the available quantum computing capability, then the resulting sub-problem is solved by quantum systems. This is the crux of Algorithm 2.

4   Conclusion

This paper proposed an approach to address the gap between the limited current capabilities of quantum computers and the minimal computational requirements of typical practical applications. It argues that quantum computational techniques will be better adopted if there exists a flexible computational technique that adapts itself to use the currently available quantum capability (instead of demanding quantum resources which may not be available commercially in foreseeable future). If this core premise of the paper is eventually supported by the results of the ongoing (in progress) investigations, then several interesting possibilities arise. Our specific interest is in commercial/industrial problems where the branch-and-bound or dynamic programming approaches do not find any evident branch dominance criterion or any implicit enumeration possibility easily. This typically happens when it is not possible to determine the objective of value of partially explored (intermediate) nodes and a deeper enumeration of nodes is essential. A substantial contribution to the existing body of research would be made by cases where the individual leaf nodes are complex for evaluation by classical computations but still amenable to quantum systems.

Acknowledgements. This work has been supported by the Academy of Finland (project DEQSE 349945) and Business Finland (project TORQS 8582/31/2022).

References

1. Daley, A.J., et al.: Practical quantum advantage in quantum simulation. Nature **607**(7920), 667–676 (2022)
2. Xiao, T., Zhai, X., Wu, X., Fan, J., Zeng, G.: Practical advantage of quantum machine learning in ghost imaging. Commun. Phys. **6**(1), 171 (2023)
3. Ferguson, R.R., Dellantonio, L., Balushi, A.A., Jansen, K., Dür, W., Muschik, C.A.: Measurement-based variational quantum eigensolver. Phys. Rev. Lett. **126**, 220501 (2021)
4. Glos, A., Kokainis, M., Mori, R., Vihrovs, J.: Quantum speedups for dynamic programming on n-dimensional lattice graphs. arXiv preprint arXiv:2104.14384 (2021)
5. Jiang, L., Taylor, J.M., Khaneja, N., Lukin, M.D.: Optimal approach to quantum communication using dynamic programming. Proc. Natl. Acad. Sci. **104**(44), 17291–17296 (2007)
6. Grover, L.K.: A fast quantum mechanical algorithm for database search. In: Proceedings of the Twenty-Eighth Annual ACM symposium on Theory of computing, pp. 212–219 (1996)

Quantum Algorithm Cards: Streamlining the Development of Hybrid Classical-Quantum Applications

Vlad Stirbu$^{(\boxtimes)}$ and Majid Haghparast

University of Jyväskylä, Jyväskylä, Finland
{vlad.a.stirbu,majid.m.haghparast}@jyu.fi

Abstract. The emergence of quantum computing proposes a revolutionary paradigm that can radically transform numerous scientific and industrial application domains. The ability of quantum computers to scale computations implies better performance and efficiency for certain algorithmic tasks than current computers provide. However, to gain benefit from such improvement, quantum computers must be integrated with existing software systems, a process that is not straightforward. In this paper, we investigate challenges that emerge when building larger hybrid classical-quantum computers and introduce the Quantum Algorithm Card (QAC) concept, an approach that could be employed to facilitate the decision making process around quantum technology.

Keywords: Quantum software · software architecture · software development life-cycle · developer's experience · quantum algorithm cards (QACs)

1 Introduction

Quantum computers have demonstrated the potential to revolutionize various fields, including cryptography, drug discovery, materials science, and machine learning, by leveraging the principles of quantum mechanics. However, the current generation of quantum computers, known as noisy intermediate-scale quantum (NISQ) computers, suffer from noise and errors, making them challenging to operate. Additionally, the development of quantum algorithms requires specialized knowledge not readily available to the majority of software professionals. These factors pose a significant entry barrier to leveraging the unique capabilities of quantum systems.

For the existing base of business applications, classical computing has already proven its capabilities across a diverse range of solutions. However, some of the computations they must perform can be accelerated with quantum computing, much like GPUs are used today. Therefore, quantum systems should not function in isolation, but they must coexist and inter-operate with classical systems.

© The Author(s), under exclusive license to Springer Nature Switzerland AG 2024
R. Kadgien et al. (Eds.): PROFES 2023, LNCS 14484, pp. 125–130, 2024.
https://doi.org/10.1007/978-3-031-49269-3_13

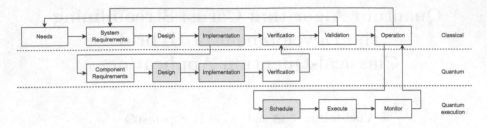

Fig. 1. Software development lifecycle of a hybrid classical-quantum system [1].

To this end, software architects play a crucial role in achieving seamless integration while simultaneously designing systems that effectively meet the unique requirements of businesses.

To address the challenges associated with this integration, this paper focuses on designing hybrid systems that integrate quantum and classical computing, aiming to overcome architectural, design, and operational hurdles. In doing so, we look at the software development lifestyle, the technology stack of hybrid classic-quantum systems, and deployment techniques used today. As a concrete contribution, we propose *quantum algorithm cards* as a mechanism to support decision making process related to quantum technology during the development and deployment of hybrid classic-quantum applications.

The rest of the paper is organized as follows. In Sect. 2, we provide the necessary background for the paper. In Sect. 3, we address architectural concerns associated with the development and deployment of hybrid classic-quantum applications. In Sect. 4, we introduce the concept of quantum algorithm cards in detail. The discussion and future plans are drawn in Sect. 5.

2   Background

The software development life-cycle (SDLC) of hybrid classic-quantum applications consists of a multi-faceted approach, as depicted in Fig. 1. At the top level, the classical software development process starts by identifying user needs and deriving them into system requirements. These requirements are transformed into a design and implemented. The result is verified against the requirements and validated against user needs. Once the software system enters the operational phase, any detected anomalies are used to identify potential new system requirements, if necessary. A dedicated track for quantum components is followed within the SDLC [2], specific to the implementation of quantum technology. The requirements for these components are converted into a design, which is subsequently implemented on classic computers, verified on simulators or real quantum hardware, and integrated into the larger software system. During the operational phase, the quantum software components are executed on real hardware. Scheduling ensures efficient utilization of scarce quantum hardware, while monitoring capabilities enable the detection of anomalies throughout the process.

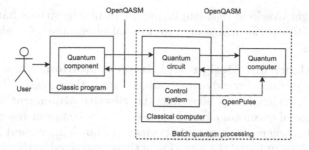

Fig. 2. Quantum computing model: components and interfaces

A typical hybrid classic-quantum software system is understood as a classical program that has one or more software components that are implemented using quantum technology, as depicted in Fig. 2. A quantum component utilizes quantum algorithms [3], that are transformed into quantum circuits using a toolkit like Cirq[1] or Qiskit[2]. The quantum circuit describes quantum computations in a machine-independent language using quantum assembly (QASM) [4]. This circuit is translated by a computer that controls the quantum computer in a machine specific circuit and a sequence of operations, such as pulses [5], that control the individual hardware qubits. The translation process, implemented using quantum compilers, encompasses supplementary actions like breaking down quantum gates, optimizing quantum circuits, and providing fault-tolerant iterations of the circuit. Further, the concept of distributed quantum computers [6], which interlink multiple distinct quantum machines through quantum communication networks, emerges as a potential solution to amplify the available quantum volume beyond what is possible using a single quantum computer. Nevertheless, the intricacies inherent in the distributed quantum computers remain hidden from users, as compilers aware of the distributed architecture of the target system shield them from such complexities. In essence, the quantum compiler plays a vital role in achieving the effective execution of generic quantum circuits on existing physical hardware platforms, making the compilers an active research area in quantum computing [7].

3   Architectural and Operational Concerns

This section highlights the SDLC stages and the key challenges can be observed while developing hybrid classic-quantum applications.

Quantum Advantage Awareness. In accordance with the hybrid classic-quantum SDLC, it becomes evident that during the decomposition of the system into smaller software components, a team with limited quantum technology

---

[1] https://quantumai.google/cirq.
[2] https://qiskit.org.

knowledge might overlook that employing quantum algorithms have the capacity to surpass the performance of conventional alternatives for algorithmically intensive tasks.

Quantum Algorithm Design and Implementation. Upon determining the possibility of quantum advantage aligned with their needs, the team often encounters a knowledge gap hindering the effective attainment of this objective. The design of quantum algorithms necessitates comprehension of quantum mechanical phenomena such as superposition, entanglement, and interference - concepts that can confound the intuition of those untrained in the field. Although well-resourced teams will likely have a *quantum scientist* specialty, similar to the data scientist role in artificial intelligence, this cannot be assumed to be generally available. This challenge leaves mainstream developers grappling to identify the optimal algorithms for their tasks. Ultimately, the team resorts to selecting algorithms bundled with widely-used quantum libraries.

Availability and Cost of Quantum Hardware. Upon successful implementation of the components and confirmation of quantum advantage, the team faces the task of selecting suitable hardware for executing the quantum tasks efficiently. This decision necessitates a comprehensive grasp of the most fitting qubit implementation technology, contingent on the interconnections among the qubits within the generic quantum circuit. While quantum compilers have the capability to convert the initial circuit into a version optimized for the specific machine, the considerations of hardware availability and associated expenses remain pivotal factors to be addressed for each application's context.

4   Quantum Algorithm Card Proposal

Addressing the previously highlighted architectural and operational considerations, our proposal recommends incorporating a Quantum Algorithm Card (QAC) in conjunction with quantum algorithm implementations. This artifact purpose is two fold: first, it serves as a repository for insights into the algorithm's implementation, and secondly, it conveys critical information for the users that rely on the implementation to realize the application specific needs. As a starting point, the QAC contains the following sections: the *overview* containing administrative information and high level overview of the algorithm purpose, the *intended purpose* describes the tasks for which the algorithm provide optimal performance, the *usage details* conveys information about how the implementation can be used and integrated into a larger system, the *performance metrics* includes information that is useful to evaluate the results of the algorithm and monitoring for deviations, the *limitations* conveys the known situations for which the use of the algorithm is not suitable, the *reference* refers to the canonical document that introduced the algorithm, and, finally, the *caveats* should include relevant information that the user should be aware. Table 1 provides an outline of the proposed QAC elements, the corresponding content and the recipients of the information. It's important to note that these elements are not exhaustive and can be tailored to suit the specifics of each corresponding quantum algorithm.

Table 1. Quantum algorithm card: elements, content and recipients (e.g. T - technology management and architects, D - software developers, O - operations)

Quantum Algorithm Card		
Element	Description	Target
Overview	- Provider/designer/maintainer information - Brief description of the algorithm's purpose, key features and functionalities - Algorithm's high-level architecture or approach, complexity	T D O
Intended use	- Clear description of the tasks the algorithm is designed for - Specific scenarios for which the quantum algorithm is intended	T
Usage details	- Information about algorithm usage, e.g. inputs and outputs - Quantum volume needed to run the algorithm	D O
Performance metrics	- Metrics and explanations used to evaluate the algorithm's performance - Decision thresholds, variation approaches, and any relevant quantitative measures	T O
Limitations	- Clear articulation of the algorithm's limitations and potential failure modes - Known scenarios where the algorithm might not perform well or could provide incorrect results	T D
References	- Citations to relevant research papers and resources	T D
Caveats	- Situations that users should avoid	D

5 Discussion and Future Work

Serving as a facilitator, the QAC artifact aims to enhance communication across common specializations within the team to support *decision making*. For example, technology managers and architects need specific information during the high-level implementation phase; software engineers need to know how the integrate the quantum technology into the larger classical system; operations needs to know how to execute and monitor the quantum components in production environment. Consequently, it is imperative that the card's content is conveyed in a language that is easily comprehensible by the intended audience, which are users and not developers of quantum technology.

The initial evaluation of the concept was performed, as an internal exercise based on a paper prototype [8] of Grover' search algorithm [9], on a target group that has both classic and quantum software development skills. The concept was found to be useful, especially for the developers that have artificial intelligence and machine learning background, as they were already familiar with similar concepts like Model Cards [10], and Data Cards [11]. However, as the classic and quantum disciplines are rather different, there is a fine line that needs to the considered carefully when deciding the depth of content about the quantum algorithm should be included, otherwise the card becomes a communication impediment rather than facilitator.

Further work is needed to validate the concept with external target groups. We are also planning to develop a Python toolkit that aims to streamline the collection of information included, and to automate the generation of QACs.

The Quantum Algorithm Cards Toolkit (QACT) will enable the developers and implementers of quantum algorithms share their metadata and metrics with developers, researchers, and other stakeholders.

Acknowledgement. This work has been supported by the Academy of Finland (project DEQSE 349945) and Business Finland (project TORQS 8582/31/2022).

References

1. Stirbu, V., Haghparast, M., Waseem, M., Dayama, N., Mikkonen, T.: Full-stack quantum software in practice: ecosystem, stakeholders and challenges. arXiv preprint arXiv:2307.16345 (2023)
2. Weder, B., Barzen, J., Leymann, F., Vietz, D.: Quantum software development lifecycle. In: Serrano, M.A., Pérez-Castillo, R., Piattini, M. (eds.) Quantum Software Engineering, pp. 61–83. Springer, Cham (2022). https://doi.org/10.1007/978-3-031-05324-5_4
3. Montanaro, A.: Quantum algorithms: an overview. NPJ Quantum Inf. **2**, 15023 (2016)
4. Cross, A., et al.: OpenQASM 3: a broader and deeper quantum assembly language. ACM Trans. Quantum Comput. **3**, 1–50 (2022)
5. Alexander, T., et al.: Qiskit pulse: programming quantum computers through the cloud with pulses. Quantum Sci. Technol. **5**, 044006 (2020)
6. Cuomo, D., Caleffi, M., Cacciapuoti, A.S.: Towards a distributed quantum computing ecosystem. IET Quantum Commun. **1**(1), 3–8 (2020)
7. Haghparast, M., Mikkonen, T., Nurminen, J.K., Stirbu, V.: Quantum software engineering challenges from developers' perspective: mapping research challenges to the proposed workflow model. arXiv preprint arXiv:2308.01141 (2023)
8. Stirbu, V., Haghparast, M.: Quantum Algorithm Card for Grover Search Algorithm (2023). https://doi.org/10.5281/zenodo.8238667
9. Grover, L.K.: A fast quantum mechanical algorithm for database search. In: Proceedings of the Twenty-Eighth Annual ACM Symposium on Theory of Computing, pp. 212–219 (1996)
10. Mitchell, M., et al.: Model cards for model reporting. In: Proceedings of the Conference on Fairness, Accountability, and Transparency, FAT* 2019, pp. 220–229. Association for Computing Machinery, New York (2019)
11. Pushkarna, M., Zaldivar, A., Kjartansson, O.: Data cards: purposeful and transparent dataset documentation for responsible AI. In: Proceedings of the 2022 ACM Conference on Fairness, Accountability, and Transparency, FAccT 2022, pp. 1776–1826. Association for Computing Machinery, New York (2022)

Doctoral Symposium

Simulation-Based Safety Testing of Automated Driving Systems

Fauzia Khan[✉][iD], Hina Anwar[iD], and Dietmar Pfahl[iD]

University of Tartu, Narva mnt 18, 51009 Tartu, Estonia
{fauzia.khan,hina.anwar,dietmar.pfahl}@ut.ee

Abstract. An Automated Driving System (ADS) must undergo comprehensive safety testing before receiving a road permit. Since it is not clear what exactly constitutes sufficient safety for an ADS, one could assume that an ADS is safe enough if it is at least as safe as a Human Driven Vehicle (HDV). Simulation-based testing is a cost-effective way to check the safety of an ADS. My goal is to develop an approach to compare the safety behavior of ADS and HDV using simulation. This comparison aims to quantify the advantages and disadvantages of ADS compared to HDV. Additionally, I aim to develop a process for selecting specific scenarios that contribute to building trust in the accuracy and reliability of simulation results. This involves defining performance criteria against which the behavior of an ADS in the simulator is compared to that of a HDV. Furthermore, I aim to translate the performance advantages or disadvantages observed in simulated ADS behavior into real-world safety-critical traffic scenarios.

Keywords: Autonomous Driving System (ADS) · Human Driven Vehicle (HDV) · Simulation-based Testing · Safety Testing · Scenario Selection

1 Motivation and Problem Statement

The primary motivation for safety testing of an ADS is to ensure public road safety, build trust, mitigate risks, and continuously improve driving. The automotive industry and researchers are trying hard to establish the appropriate level of trust in an ADS to be accepted by human passengers and drivers of traditional cars (non-ADS).

The aim of my Ph.D. project is to quantify the advantages and disadvantages of an ADS compared to a typical HDV using simulation-based safety testing and to lay the foundation for making recommendations to transportation/traffic regulators on how to either adapt the traffic environment or traffic rules to mitigate identified ADS disadvantages in cases where this is possible and easier to achieve

Supported by Estonian Research Council grant PRG1226, Bolt Technology OÜ grant, and the Estonian state stipend for doctoral studies.

R. Kadgien et al. (Eds.): PROFES 2023, LNCS 14484, pp. 133–138, 2024.
https://doi.org/10.1007/978-3-031-49269-3_14

than to improve the ADS performance. By analyzing available quantitative data, insights can be gained to inform regulatory adjustments that effectively neutralize identified ADS disadvantages.

While simulation is a cost-effective approach to test ADS safety and to quantify its advantages and disadvantages over an HDV, what exact conclusions can be drawn from simulation-based testing is not straightforward. It is important to ensure that simulated sensors, hardware, software, as well as scenarios closely resemble those of real-world counterparts.

Additionally, the complexity of driving tasks and the potentially infinite number of driving environments and situations yield an exponentially growing number of scenarios in which an ADS may be tested.

Finally, quantifying ADS disadvantages compared to a typical HDV in the real world poses another challenge arising from the lack of relevant (pre-)crash data of HDVs. The absence of such data makes it difficult to translate any unfavourable ADS behavior observed in simulations to problems that an ADS would create in the real-world while an HDV typically would not.

2   Research Goals

The research goals of my Ph.D. thesis are as follows:

- **RG1 [Scenarios]:** To develop a process for prioritizing and selecting scenarios for ADS safety testing.
- **RG2 [Simulation Environment]:** To create a simulation environment and implement the selected scenarios within a simulator.
- **RG3 [Experiments]:** To execute the experiments in the simulator and assess the performance of an ADS as compared to an HDV in scenarios.

3   Approach and Planned Contributions

The research approach is divided into five key steps as shown in Fig. 1: (i) prioritizing and selecting test scenarios (ii) creating simulation models capturing the behavior of an ADS and a HDV, (iii) running simulations against the selected test scenarios, (iv) defining criteria for performance evaluation (v) and evaluating the performance of both ADS and HDV.

To initiate my research, I conducted a survey to gather insights on the methods used by both research and industrial experts for the safety testing of ADS. This review aims to shed light on the (i) ADS types, (ii) safety features, (iii) testing methods, and (iv) tools and datasets used in the safety testing of ADS. To achieve above mentioned RGs, I present the planned contributions as follows.

Contribution 1: This contribution aims to achieve **RG1**, i.e., prioritizing and selecting scenarios for the safety testing of an ADS. Defining scenarios includes the representation and combination of various factors such as scenery, traffic, road objects, environment, road geometry, and maneuvers, along with the

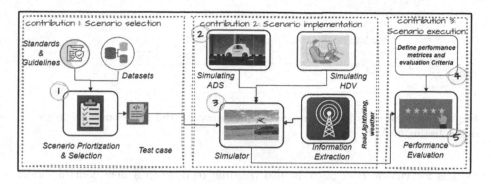

Fig. 1. Proposed Approach

increasing complexity and uncertainty of driving tasks. Since it is impossible to simulate every possible scenario [5,6], I am working on defining a process for prioritizing and selecting scenarios from the existing lists of scenarios. The aim is to refine the scope of testing scenarios and focus on the most representative and critical ones for evaluating ADS safety. Initially, a pre-existing scenario catalog from a reputable organization is selected. A set of straightforward scenarios are selected based on the Operational Design Domain (ODD) relevant to the city of Tartu; then, the remaining scenarios are grouped based on similarities in critical actions of the ego vehicle[1] or target object (vehicles, pedestrians cyclist, etc.). After formulation of scenario groups, the scenario groups are prioritized using real-world data, focusing on those encountered frequently in real driving situations. Duplicates are removed. Furthermore, scenarios that are not feasible to implement in the simulation environment's limitations are filtered out. In each scenario group, a scoring technique is used to assign scores based on the frequency of elements, i.e., (actors, driving maneuvers, weather, and lighting conditions) found in road accident datasets. Ultimately, the highest-scored scenario in each priority group is selected for ADS testing through simulation. Figure 2 shows the overview of the proposed process for prioritization and selection of scenarios for safety testing of ADS. This contribution will help to narrow down the range of scenarios to be tested and focus on those that are most critical for evaluating ADS performance.

Contribution 2: This contribution aims to achieve **RG2**. I will create a realistic simulation environment using CARLA[2] and implement the selected scenarios from contribution 1 to analyze the behavior of an ADS and HDV through selected scenarios. I chose ScenarioRunner[3] for implementing the scenarios in CARLA as it can describe complex scenarios and entity movements, including vehicles and pedestrians. Furthermore, to stimulate ADS, Python API[4] offers various

---

[1] The ADS under test.

[2] https://carla.org/.

[3] https://carla-scenariorunner.readthedocs.io/en/latest/.

[4] https://carla.readthedocs.io/en/latest/python_api/.

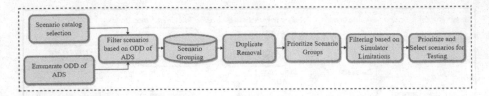

Fig. 2. Overview of proposed process for prioritization and selection of scenarios for safety testing of ADS

models for vehicle control; it is also possible to develop a new control model from scratch. Using Python API, the environment and vehicles can manipulate. The CARLA ROS bridge[5] also facilitates the connection between CARLA and a third-party ROS-based control system for the ego vehicle. My preference is to utilize the ROS bridge to interface with Autoware Mini[6]. Moreover, CARLA has a human-like driving behavior model based on real-world data distribution, e.g., aggressive, distracted, naturalistic, and low aggressive drivers, which could be used for HDV simulation. Contribution 2 provides a controlled simulation environment and valuable insights into the comparative performance of ADS and HDV, ultimately contributing to a better understanding of the strengths and weaknesses of ADS in various real-world driving situations.

Contribution 3: This contribution aims to achieve **RG3**. I will define the criteria and metrics for evaluating and assessing the performance of ADS and HDV simulated in contribution 2, focusing on safety, e.g., by counting the number of collisions, near-miss incidents, or violations of traffic regulations.

4   Preliminary Results of Contribution 1

For prioritization and selection of scenarios for ADS safety testing, I apply the proposed process to two existing scenarios catalogs. The first catalog is provided by the Land Transport Authority of Singapore[7] and the second catalog is published by the US Department of Transportation[8]. The first catalog consists of 67 diverse real-world traffic scenarios and the second catalog consists of 44 pre-crash scenarios, specifically capturing the situations and conditions leading up to a traffic accident or collision. The total number of scenarios in both selected catalogs is 111. Twenty-one scenarios are excluded based on the ODD specific to ADS. The remaining scenarios are categorized into fifteen distinct groups. Nine duplicated scenarios are removed, and eight scenario groups are prioritized based on crash statistics retrieved from real-world data. Considering CARLA simulators' limitations, six scenario groups from the prioritized containing fifty-one scenarios for testing ADS in the CARLA simulator.

---

[5] https://carla.readthedocs.io/projects/ros-bridge/en/latest/.

[6] https://github.com/UT-ADL/autoware_mini.

[7] List of scenarios - Land Transport Authority of Singapore.

[8] List of scenarios - US Department of Transportation - Table 1.

5 Related Work

Several studies performed the safety testing of ADS using open-road [3,4,7,11] test beds [1,9] and simulators [2,8,10,12]. Due to space limitations, we only include here the studies that perform ADS safety testing using simulation. Matthew et al. [10] presented a simulation framework based on an adaptive sampling method to test an entire ADS. Jha et al. [8] proposed a fault injection tool that systematically injects faults into the hardware and software of an ADS to evaluate safety and reliability. Ben et al. [2] presented an approach to test ADS in a simulation environment (Simulink) using multi-objective search and surrogate models based on a neural network to identify critical test cases regarding an ADS behavior. Wicker et al. [12] performed black box testing to evaluate the robustness of neural networks against adversarial attacks in traffic sign recognition in self-driving cars. My work is different from existing work in simulation-based ADS safety testing by adopting a black-box perspective when observing the behavior of the ADS. The focus is primarily on identifying ADS behavior that deviates from that of HDVs, accounting for positive and negative distinctions. My Ph.D. project is expected to be completed by August 2025.

Acknowledgements. This research was partly funded by the Austrian BMK, BMAW, and State of Upper Austria under the SCCH competence center INTEGRATE [(FFG grant 892418)], the Estonian Research Council (grant PRG1226), Bolt Technology OÜ, and the Estonian state stipend for doctoral studies.

References

1. Althoff, M., Dolan, J.M.: Online verification of automated road vehicles using reachability analysis. IEEE Trans. Robot. **30**(4), 903–918 (2014)
2. Ben Abdessalem, R., Nejati, S., Briand, L.C., Stifter, T.: Testing advanced driver assistance systems using multi-objective search and neural networks. In: Proceedings of the 31st IEEE/ACM International Conference on Automated Software Engineering, pp. 63–74 (2016)
3. Broggi, A., et al.: Extensive tests of autonomous driving technologies. IEEE Trans. Intell. Transp. Syst. **14**(3), 1403–1415 (2013)
4. Broggi, A., Cerri, P., Felisa, M., Laghi, M.C., Mazzei, L., Porta, P.P.: The VisLab intercontinental autonomous challenge: an extensive test for a platoon of intelligent vehicles. Int. J. Veh. Auton. Syst. **10**(3), 147–164 (2012)
5. Chen, Z., He, F., Yin, Y., Du, Y.: Optimal design of autonomous vehicle zones in transportation networks. Transp. Res. Part B: Methodological **99**, 44–61 (2017)
6. Duarte, F., Ratti, C.: The impact of autonomous vehicles on cities: a review. J. Urban Technol. **25**(4), 3–18 (2018)
7. Funke, J., et al.: Up to the limits: autonomous Audi TTS. In: 2012 IEEE Intelligent Vehicles Symposium, pp. 541–547. IEEE (2012)
8. Jha, S., et al.: Kayotee: a fault injection-based system to assess the safety and reliability of autonomous vehicles to faults and errors. arXiv preprint arXiv:1907.01024 (2019)

9. Nieuwenhuijze, M.R., van Keulen, T., Öncü, S., Bonsen, B., Nijmeijer, H.: Cooperative driving with a heavy-duty truck in mixed traffic: experimental results. IEEE Trans. Intell. Transp. Syst. **13**(3), 1026–1032 (2012)
10. O'Kelly, M., Sinha, A., Namkoong, H., Tedrake, R., Duchi, J.C.: Scalable end-to-end autonomous vehicle testing via rare-event simulation. In: Advances in Neural Information Processing Systems, vol. 31 (2018)
11. Ploeg, J., Scheepers, B.T., Van Nunen, E., Van de Wouw, N., Nijmeijer, H.: Design and experimental evaluation of cooperative adaptive cruise control. In: 2011 14th International IEEE Conference on Intelligent Transportation Systems (ITSC), pp. 260–265. IEEE (2011)
12. Wicker, M., Huang, X., Kwiatkowska, M.: Feature-guided black-box safety testing of deep neural networks. In: Beyer, D., Huisman, M. (eds.) TACAS 2018. LNCS, vol. 10805, pp. 408–426. Springer, Cham (2018). https://doi.org/10.1007/978-3-319-89960-2_22

Utilization of Machine Learning for the Detection of Self-admitted Vulnerabilities

Moritz Mock[✉][iD]

Faculty of Engineering, Free University of Bozen-Bolzano, Bolzano, Italy
moritz.mock@student.unibz.it

Abstract. Motivation: Technical debt is a metaphor that describes not-quite-right code introduced for short-term needs. Developers are aware of it and admit it in source code comments, which is called Self-Admitted Technical Debt (SATD). Therefore, SATD indicates weak code that developers are aware of. **Problem statement:** Inspecting source code is time-consuming; automatically inspecting source code for its vulnerabilities is a crucial aspect of developing software. It helps practitioners reduce the time-consuming process and focus on vulnerable aspects of the source code. **Proposal:** Accurately identify and better understand the semantics of self-admitted technical debt (SATD) by leveraging NLP and NL-PL approaches to detect vulnerabilities and the related SATD. Finally, a CI/CD pipeline will be proposed to make the vulnerability discovery process easily accessible to practitioners.

Keywords: Software Vulnerabilities · Code Comments · Self-Admitted Technical Debt · Machine Learning · NL-PL

1 Introduction

Technical debt (TD) is a metaphor introduced by Cunningham [4], which describes the short-term benefits of not-quite-right code, such as being able to deliver the code faster. In the paper of Bavota *et al.* [2], it was illustrated that the negative impact of TD increases over time and that the payback of technical debt should not be postponed for too long. In 2014, the concept of self-admitted technical debt (SATD) was introduced by Potdar and Shihab [15], which refers to comments left behind by developers to indicate that the code is not quite right. Furthermore, they have presented 62 patterns which can identify SATD. Due to the patterns' high precision and low accuracy, in recent years, different machine learning (ML) approaches (e.g., [12,16,19]) have been employed to detect SATD. With the ML approach of [16], they were able to identify more than 700 patterns, which, according to their approach, indicate SATD.

For the part of vulnerability detection, many static analysis tools (e.g., Cppcheck and Flawfinder) and ML approaches (e.g., [9,11,13]) already exist for

R. Kadgien et al. (Eds.): PROFES 2023, LNCS 14484, pp. 139–145, 2024.
https://doi.org/10.1007/978-3-031-49269-3_15

all kinds of programming languages (PL) and vulnerability types. To the best of our knowledge, no tool leverages both concepts by connecting them besides our own tool WeakSATD Russo *et al.* [17]. Furthermore, the Common Weakness Enumeration (CWE[1]) and the Common Vulnerability and Exposure (CVE[2]) repositories provide a large set of abstract and real-world vulnerability instances, respectively, both of which can be employed for machine-learning-related tasks.

This paper proposes to foster the understanding of SATD and its semantics in related comments. Furthermore, the investigation of the correlation between SATD and vulnerabilities. An annotated dataset for SATD and vulnerabilities will also be presented, focusing on CWE-related vulnerabilities. For which different Natural Language Processing (NLP) and Natural Language Programming Language (NL-PL) techniques are employed. The machine learner should be able to detect the vulnerability, indicate the affected line, and provide practitioners with easy-to-understand assistance on how to fix the vulnerability. Lastly, an integration in a continuous integration pipeline (CI/CD) is foreseen.

The rest of this doctorate proposal includes state-of-the-art SATD and vulnerability detection, which is presented in Sect. 2. It is followed by the Sect. 3, illustrating the proposal. The conclusion and future work are presented in Sect. 4, which additionally contains the timeline for the PhD.

2   State of the Art

We have reviewed the existing literature according to two dimensions: (i) SATD and (ii) vulnerability detection. In the following, we give an overview of them.

SATD: For SATD comment detection, the two primary approaches advocated in the literature are pattern-based and machine learning. Potdar and Shihab [15] presented the fundamental paper for the pattern-based approach. They defined 62 unique SATD patterns by examining 101,762 comments over four open-source projects (Eclipse, Chromium OS, ArgoUML and Apache httpd). Different approaches for the detection of SATD have been studied (e.g., [1,10,12,19]). Hung *et al.* [12] leveraged a Multinomial Naive Bayes approach for the detection of SATD, for which they used the manually annotated dataset of 62566 Java comments, containing 4071 SATD comments, presented by Maldonado *et al.* [14]. Ren *et al.* [16] proposed a Convolutional Neural Network (CNN) to detect SATD with an average F1 of 0.766 over eight open-source projects annotated by Maldonado *et al.* [14]. Furthermore, they have investigated which keywords, besides the 62 patterns from Potdar and Shihab [15], have statistical significance for SATD identification. With that approach, they were able to propose 700 patterns for SATD detection. In the study of Guo *et al.* [10], the CNN approach of Ren *et al.* [16] was investigated. They could not replicate the initially

---

[1] https://cve.mitre.org/.
[2] https://cwe.mitre.org/.

obtained F1 score; their result was 0.654 for the F1, effectively being 0.112 points lower than the initial findings. In the recently published study of Aiken *et al.* [1], BERT [5] was employed to predict SATD in the dataset of Maldonado *et al.* [14]. They have achieved an average F1 of 0.858 in a cross-project evaluation. Furthermore, new sets of patterns have been introduced and used for the detection of SATD, which differ from the original proposed 62 patterns [6,10,16]. Guo *et al.* [10] proposed a set of patterns consisting of "TODO", "HACK", "XXX", and "FIXME", which they called Matches task Annotation Tags (MAT). Their idea is that developers are particularly prone to use those four patterns to remind themselves, as those patterns are automatically highlighted in the most common Integrated Development Environments (IDSs).

Vulnerability: The repository of CWE provides an in-depth view of more than 400 instances of source-code-related vulnerabilities, which are held quite general and abstract without leveraging on real-world examples. Most of them contain an abstract source-code example with steps on how to mitigate the vulnerability besides the textual description. In contrast, the CVE repository is a collection of vulnerabilities taken from real-world applications. Where possible, they contain the link to the corresponding commit-ID, which fixed the vulnerability. The dataset Big-Vul presented by Fan *et al.* [7] provided 3754 vulnerabilities of 91 different vulnerability types. Big-Vul was used in the study of Fu *et al.* [9] in which LineVul was presented, a transformer-based application leveraging on CodeBERT [8], to perform line-level predictions of vulnerabilities. With their approach, they obtained an F1 score of 0.91. Devign was proposed by Zhuo *et al.* [18], a Graph Neural Network (GNN) for the vulnerability of the programming language C for the detection they are leveraging on the Abstract Syntax Tree representation of source code. For their approach, they manually annotated vulnerabilities from four large open-source projects: FFMpeg, Wireshark, Linux Kernel, and QEMU. The current SOTA leverages many individually created datasets, which has only changed recently with the introduction of easy-to-use datasets such as Big-Vul [7] and Devign [18]. Especially the part of explanatory vulnerability detection was not explored at all. Fu *et al.* [9] went in this direction by implementing a tool, LineVul, which is capable of line-level vulnerability prediction. However, they lack in the part of providing an explanation of *how to fix* the detected vulnerability. Chakraborty *et al.* [3] studied the capability of state-of-the-art machine learning vulnerability detection approaches towards real-world datasets. To perform their evaluation, they used the published dataset of Devign [18] and a curated dataset from Chromium and Debian. They have found that the existing datasets are rather too simple and not realistic enough, so the machine learners trained on them may not achieve the expected results.

3   Proposal

This proposal for automated self-admitted vulnerabilities detection is illustrated in the following five major steps: ① **Dataset annotation**, ② **SATD detection, ③ **vulnerability detection**, ④ **combining the obtained results of SATD and vulnerability detection**, and ⑤ **CI/CD pipeline**.

① For the annotation of a dataset, our previously presented tool, WeakSATD [17], will be employed, as it gives us line-level vulnerability classification, which can be leveraged in the following steps of the proposal.

② The detection of self-admitted technical debt has already been explored in literature and has been recognised. However, there is some disagreement on which patterns indicate SATD. This step is split into two parts; the first step provides a better understanding of what characterises the semantics of a SATD as such and whether there is a classification of a SATD comment as an indicator of a security breach. Traditional NLP and NL-PL approaches will be used, of which the second is underrepresented in the current literature. In the second step, a machine learner will label the source code as vulnerable and generate comments, potentially SATD, for it to further emphasise its vulnerability for developers.

③ For the detection of vulnerabilities, transformer-based machine-learning approaches with pre-trained models for source code understanding will be employed. Additionally, the capability of such machine learners is studied for the recommendation of mitigation steps for vulnerabilities to practitioners.

④ Combining both SATD and vulnerability detection approaches has not yet been explored in the literature. We hope to increase the measured results by leveraging both concepts, SATD and vulnerability detection and to increase the efficiency of a machine learner by reducing the needed computational power.

⑤ The existing literature highly focuses on finding the best approach to detecting SATD or vulnerabilities, and only a limited number of tools are available for integrating them into the development process of source code. Various approaches can be taken for this step, such as a command line interface (CLI) or an IDE plugin. With the advent of CI/CD pipelines since the introduction of Github Actions, these have become more common due to their asynchronous nature. Giving practitioners the possibility to evaluate the source code detached from their development process will increase the productivity of a practitioner and reduce the vulnerabilities in the code.

4   Conclusion and Future Work

Conclusion: This doctoral proposal suggests the implementation of a CI/CD pipeline to make it as easy as possible for practitioners to access a SATD and vulnerability detection tool. Furthermore, a gap in the detection of SATD was identified with its proposed exploration of NLP and NL-PL approaches to extract a more in-depth understanding of the semantics of SATD and its connection to security breaches. Lastly, the absence of a dataset annotated at the line level for vulnerabilities was identified. A connection with CWE helps the practitioner find clear guidance in the explanation of the vulnerability, how to fix it, and how to mitigate it in the future can be retrieved. **Future work:** After each step, but especially after step ② and ③ of the proposal, practitioners will be interviewed to understand how they perceive the labelling of the machine learner. As well as to showcase step ⑤ to understand if the foreseen solution with the CI/CD pipeline is applicable in their development process. **Timeline:** In November 2023, the three-year PhD of Advanced-Systems Engineering started. Figure 1 illustrates the study's full timeline, with the defence in 2027. This proposal was presented at the phase of the literature review of the PhD program.

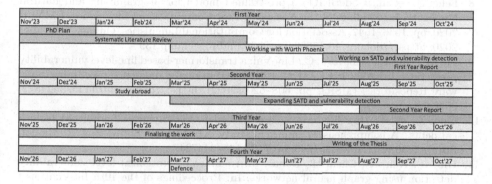

Fig. 1. Timeline of the PhD study

Acknowledgement. I sincerely thank my advisor, Prof. Barbara Russo, Full Professor at the Free University of Bozan-Bolzano, for her support during my academic journey.

References

1. Aiken, W., Mvula, P.K., Branco, P., Jourdan, G., Sabetzadeh, M., Viktor, H.: Measuring improvement of F1-scores in detection of self-admitted technical debt. In: 2023 ACM/IEEE International Conference on Technical Debt (TechDebt), pp. 37–41. IEEE Computer Society, Los Alamitos, CA, USA, May 2023. https://doi.org/10.1109/TechDebt59074.2023.00011
2. Bavota, G., Russo, B.: A large-scale empirical study on self-admitted technical debt. In: Proceedings of the 13th International Conference on Mining Software Repositories, MSR 2016, pp. 315–326. Association for Computing Machinery, New York, NY, USA (2016). https://doi.org/10.1145/2901739.2901742
3. Chakraborty, S., Krishna, R., Ding, Y., Ray, B.: Deep learning based vulnerability detection: are we there yet? IEEE Trans. Softw. Eng. **48**(09), 3280–3296 (2022). https://doi.org/10.1109/TSE.2021.3087402

4. Cunningham, W.: The WYCash portfolio management system. SIGPLAN OOPS Mess. **4**(2), 29–30 (1992). https://doi.org/10.1145/157710.157715

5. Devlin, J., Chang, M.W., Lee, K., Toutanova, K.: BERT: pre-training of deep bidirectional transformers for language understanding. arXiv preprint arXiv:1810.04805 (2018). https://doi.org/10.48550/arXiv.1810.04805

6. Ebrahimi, A.M., Oliva, G.A., Hassan, A.E.: Self-admitted technical debt in ethereum smart contracts: a large-scale exploratory study. IEEE Trans. Softw. Eng. **49**, 4304-4323 (2023). https://doi.org/10.1109/TSE.2023.3289808

7. Fan, J., Li, Y., Wang, S., Nguyen, T.N.: A C/C++ code vulnerability dataset with code changes and CVE summaries. In: Proceedings of the 17th International Conference on Mining Software Repositories, MSR 2020, pp. 508–512. Association for Computing Machinery, New York, NY, USA (2020). https://doi.org/10.1145/3379597.3387501

8. Feng, Z., et al.: CodeBERT: a pre-trained model for programming and natural languages. In: Findings of the Association for Computational Linguistics: EMNLP 2020, pp. 1536–1547. Association for Computational Linguistics, Online, November 2020. https://doi.org/10.18653/v1/2020.findings-emnlp.139

9. Fu, M., Tantithamthavorn, C.: LineVul: a transformer-based line-level vulnerability prediction. In: 2022 IEEE/ACM 19th International Conference on Mining Software Repositories (MSR), pp. 608–620 (2022). https://doi.org/10.1145/3524842.3528452

10. Guo, Z., et al.: How far have we progressed in identifying self-admitted technical debts? A comprehensive empirical study. ACM Trans. Softw. Eng. Methodol. **30**(4), 1–56 (2021). https://doi.org/10.1145/3447247

11. Hin, D., Kan, A., Chen, H., Babar, M.A.: LineVD: statement-level vulnerability detection using graph neural networks. In: Proceedings of the 19th International Conference on Mining Software Repositories, MSR 2022, pp. 596–607. Association for Computing Machinery, New York, NY, USA (2022). https://doi.org/10.1145/3524842.3527949

12. Huang, Q., Shihab, E., Xia, X., Lo, D., Li, S.: Identifying self-admitted technical debt in open source projects using text mining. Empir. Softw. Eng. **23**, 418–451 (2018). https://doi.org/10.1007/s10664-017-9522-4

13. Li, Y., Wang, S., Nguyen, T.N.: Vulnerability detection with fine-grained interpretations. In: Proceedings of the 29th ACM Joint Meeting on European Software Engineering Conference and Symposium on the Foundations of Software Engineering, ESEC/FSE 2021, pp. 292–303. Association for Computing Machinery, New York, NY, USA (2021). https://doi.org/10.1145/3468264.3468597

14. Maldonado, E.D.S., Shihab, E., Tsantalis, N.: Using natural language processing to automatically detect self-admitted technical debt. IEEE Trans. Softw. Eng. **43**(11), 1044–1062 (2017). https://doi.org/10.1109/TSE.2017.2654244

15. Potdar, A., Shihab, E.: An exploratory study on self-admitted technical debt. In: 2014 IEEE International Conference on Software Maintenance and Evolution, pp. 91–100 (2014). https://doi.org/10.1109/ICSME.2014.31

16. Ren, X., Xing, Z., Xia, X., Lo, D., Wang, X., Grundy, J.: Neural network-based detection of self-admitted technical debt: from performance to explainability. ACM Trans. Softw. Eng. Methodol. **28**(3), 1–45 (2019). https://doi.org/10.1145/3324916

17. Russo, B., Camilli, M., Mock, M.: WeakSATD: detecting weak self-admitted technical debt. In: 2022 IEEE/ACM 19th International Conference on Mining Software Repositories (MSR), pp. 448–453 (2022). https://doi.org/10.1145/3524842.3528469

18. Zhou, Y., Liu, S., Siow, J., Du, X., Liu, Y.: Devign: effective vulnerability identification by learning comprehensive program semantics via graph neural networks. Curran Associates Inc., Red Hook, NY, USA (2019). https://doi.org/10.48550/arXiv.1909.03496

19. Zhu, K., Yin, M., Zhu, D., Zhang, X., Gao, C., Jiang, J.: SCGRU: a general approach for identifying multiple classes of self-admitted technical debt with text generation oversampling. J. Syst. Softw. **195**, 111514 (2023). https://doi.org/10.1016/j.jss.2022.111514

Closing the Loop: Towards a Complete Metamorphic Testing Pipeline

Alejandra Duque-Torres[✉][ID] and Dietmar Pfahl[ID]

Institute of Computer Science, University of Tartu, Tartu, Estonia
{duquet,dietmar.pfahl}@ut.ee

Abstract. Metamorphic Testing (MT) address the test oracle problem, which arises when there are no practical means to verify the outputs of the System Under Test (SUT). Instead of just verifying individual input-output combinations, MT assesses the relations between pairs of these combinations during consecutive SUT executions; these relations are known as Metamorphic Relations (MRs). MRs delineate how outputs should adapt based on input changes. Automating MR generation is challenging because of the intrinsic connection between MRs and the SUT's domain. Furthermore, the relevance of MRs can be contingent upon specific data. Motivated by this, our research focuses on facilitating the generation and selection of MRs, defining their applicability by establishing constraints and shedding light on the factors influencing MR outcomes. Our goal is to equip testers with methods and tools that optimise the application of the MT approach.

1 Introduction

Metamorphic Testing (MT) is a software testing approach designed to address the test oracle problem. This problem emerges when the System Under Test (SUT) doesn't have an oracle or when creating one to validate the computed outputs becomes practically infeasible [7]. Unlike conventional testing techniques, MT analyses the relations between pairs of input-output combinations across consecutive executions of the SUT rather than focusing solely on verifying individual input-output combinations. Such relations are known as Metamorphic Relations (MRs). MRs specify how the outputs should vary in response to specific input changes. When an MR is violated for at least one valid test input, it indicates a potential fault within the SUT. Nevertheless, the absence of MR violations does not guarantee a fault-free SUT. A good MR must not only specify correctly the input-output relations across the valid input data space - it also must be capable of detecting incorrect program behaviour resulting from a fault in the SUT code.

Achieving full automation in the generation and selection of MRs, as well as understanding the reasons for MR outcomes-specifically discerning whether an MR violation is due to a fault in the SUT or an issue with the MR for the chosen input values is challenging for two main reasons. Firstly, MRs are closely

R. Kadgien et al. (Eds.): PROFES 2023, LNCS 14484, pp. 146–151, 2024.
https://doi.org/10.1007/978-3-031-49269-3_16

tied to the SUT's behaviour and its application domain when it comes to their generation and selection. This requires an in-depth understanding, especially for an accurate generation or selection, if a predefined set of MRs is given. While the identification of some MRs is straightforward, others require complex reasoning or in-depth domain knowledge. Secondly, MR applicability can differ across input data, *i.e.*, certain MRs might only apply to specific input data subsets. Driven by these challenges, our research aims to support the generation and selection of MRs, define relevant constraints for them, and provide clarity on the factors influencing MR outcomes. Ultimately, we seek to equip testers with tools and methodologies that optimise the MT approach's implementation.

Our research is organised into three main parts: (1) MR generation and selection, (2) MR constraint definition, and (3) evaluation and validation. In the MR generation and selection part, our research goal (RG_1) is to offer a method for MR generation and to introduce a generalised representation or domain-specific language to describe these generated MRs. For the MR constraint definition part, the goal (RG_2) is to devise a method that defines constraints on MRs based on test data and provides an explanation for MR outcomes, whether they're violations or non-violations. Lastly, in the evaluation and validation part, the goal (RG_3) is to gauge the efficacy and efficiency of the proposed methods and tools via empirical studies. In the subsequent sections of the paper, we delve deeper into the research questions, discuss the current status, and outline our planned work for each part.

2   MR Generation and Selection

To address RG_1, we pose the following research questions:

- **RQ$_{1.1}$** How do various sources, such as system specifications and domain knowledge, contribute to the identification of MRs for a targeted SUT?
- **RQ$_{1.2}$** How to transcribe generated MRs into a format that enables their systematic interpretation by test automation tools?

2.1   Ongoing Work

Inspired by open bug repositories, Xie et al. introduced METWiki, an MR database. It compiles MRs from about 110 MT applications across various domains, sourced from a comprehensive literature review on MT [12]. However, METWiki has its shortcomings. Since its 2016 release, it hasn't been updated, questioning the MRs' current relevance. Additionally, there's inconsistency in MR descriptions, complicating their comprehension and automated processing. Lastly, while MRs are sorted into eight domains, the lack of inter-domain connections hampers broader understanding and cross-domain MR utilisation.

Building upon the METWiki concept, we're currently creating an updated MR database. Our approach involves consolidating METWiki's existing MRs and acquiring additional MRs from prominent conferences and specialised workshops, such as the MET workshop at the ICSE conference. Creating this new database requires manual effort. To ensure database quality and utility, we're assessing methods for consistent MR description formatting and cross-domain categorisation. This endeavour seeks to reduce redundancy and boost database usability. Our objective is twofold: to not only integrate METWiki's current MRs but also encompass a broader spectrum of MRs presented at top conferences and workshops. This refined database will serve as a vital resource for researchers and practitioners in MT, aiding the identification and application of pertinent MRs in diverse software testing scenarios. In doing so, we aim to address $RQ_{1.1}$.

2.2   Planned Work

After completing the MR database, the next step involves devising a domain-specific language to facilitate the translation of MRs into test code through a machine-readable format. We'll leverage existing proposals [2,10,11], which provide valuable insights into creating a format that is adaptable, flexible, and compatible with various SUTs, addressing $RQ_{1.2}$.

2.3   Preliminary Achievements

To explore alternative sources for extracting MRs, we explored Blasi et al.'s work on "MeMo" [1], specifically focusing on the MR-Finder module. This module infers MRs by analysing sentences in Javadoc's comments that describe equivalent behaviours between different methods of the same class. For a detailed exploration of our study and results, please see our publication in [3].

To match a pre-defined set of MRs with the SUT, we explored the Predicting Metamorphic Relations (PMR) approach proposed by [8,9]. The idea behind PMR is to create a model that predicts whether a specific MR can be used to test a method in a newly developed SUT. We conducted a replication study on the PMR [9] to assess its generalisability across multiple programming languages [4]. We rebuilt the preprocessing and training pipeline, closely replicating the original study. Furthermore, we assessed the potential reusability of the PMR model, specifically one trained on Java methods, by determining its suitability for methods in Python and C++. Additionally, we conducted an evaluation of the PMR approach using source code metrics as an alternative to CFG for building the models [7]. For more detailed information about our replication study and extension using source code metrics, we refer the reader to our publications in [4,7].

3   MR Constrain Definition

To achieve RG_2, we must answer the following research questions:

- $RQ_{2.1}$: How to systematically differentiate between MR violations due to code faults and those stemming from MR constraints?
- $RQ_{2.2}$: How to explain the reasons for the MT verdict when using a specific MR?

3.1   Ongoing Work

We have introduced a novel approach and are currently in the process of enhancing it a test data-driven technique for constraining MRs known as MetaTrimmer [6]. Similar to PMR, we assume the availability of a predefined set of MRs. However, MetaTrimmer does not rely on labelled datasets and takes into account that an MR may only be applicable to test data with specific characteristics. MetaTrimmer encompasses three steps: (1) Test Data Generation (TD Generation), (2) MT Process, and (3) MR Analysis. The first step involves generating random test data for the SUT. In the second step, the MT Process carries out essential test data transformations based on MRs. This generates logs documenting input-output details and any MR violations encountered during the execution of both the original and transformed test data against the SUT. The third step, MR Analysis, involves manual examinations of violation and non-violation outcomes. This helps identify specific test data or ranges where the MR is relevant, enabling the derivation of constraints. Concurrently, we are developing a supporting tool for the MR Analysis step, known as MetaExploreX. Through the formalisation and assessment of MetaTrimmer, our aim is to address Research Question $RQ_{2.1}$.

3.2   Planned Work

In the next stage of our research, our focus is on automating the process of constraint derivation. Currently, the identification of constraints entails manual assessment of violation statuses, a task that can be both labour-intensive and time-consuming. Using data mining techniques, we'll analyze data related to MR violations, test data, and pertinent details to identify prevalent patterns and connections. These insights will guide us in formulating constraints that precisely outline the circumstances where MRs are valid or not. In this way, we're addressing the question of accurately capturing the applicability of MRs and answering $RQ_{2.2}$

3.3   Preliminary Achievements

We have introduced the main idea of MetaTrimmer and evaluated its effectiveness through a toy example. For more detailed information about this study, we refer the reader to our publication [5]. Furthermore, we have submitted and registered a paper in which we present the formalisation of MetaTrimmer and its evaluation on 25 Python methods and six-predefined MRs. For a detailed exploration of our study and results, please see our publication in [6]

4   Evaluation and Validation

To achieve this goal, we focus on answering the following research question:

– $RQ_{3.1}$: How well do the proposed methods perform compared to existing approaches?
– $RQ_{3.2}$: How effective are the proposed methods in finding faults?

To address the research question regarding the effectiveness of our approach ($RQ_{3.1}$), we plan to conduct a mutation testing analysis. Mutation testing involves introducing small modifications or "mutants" into the SUT and examining how well the constrained MRs can detect these mutations as faults. In order to address research question $RQ_{3.1}$, we will conduct a comprehensive comparison at every step of our research. Throughout the development and evaluation of our methods and tools, we will consistently compare their performance against baseline approaches. These baseline approaches may include existing manual MR selection methods or other fully automated approaches commonly used in the field.

5   Final Remarks

Our research offers a deep dive into MT, specifically focusing on the generation, constraint definition, and validation of MRs. By enhancing and revising existing methodologies, our work promises to provide a more structured framework for practitioners and researchers in the MT domain. Our updated MR database not only consolidates existing knowledge but also integrates recent advancements. This database, anticipated to become an invaluable asset, encapsulates a comprehensive set of MRs, fostering more rigorous and diversified MT applications. The introduction of MetaTrimmer and MetaExploreX marks a significant stride towards automation in MR analysis. By facilitating the systematic assessment of MR outcomes, these tools aim to reduce manual overhead. We believe that the results of our research will produce concrete support for software testers, offering insights into effective strategies for MR generation and constraint definition. By doing so, we aspire to contribute to the advancement of MT as a reliable and valuable testing approach, guiding future research studies and fostering continuous improvement in this field.

Acknowledgement. The research reported in this paper has been partly funded by BMK, BMAW, and the State of Upper Austria in the frame of the SCCH competence center INTEGRATE [(FFG grant no. 892418)] part of the FFG COMET Competence Centers for Excellent Technologies Programme, as well as by the European Regional Development Fund, and grant PRG1226 of the Estonian Research Council.

References

1. Blasi, A., Gorla, A., Ernst, M.D., Pezzè, M., Carzaniga, A.: MeMo: automatically identifying metamorphic relations in Javadoc comments for test automation. J. Syst. Softw. **181**, 111041 (2021)
2. Chaleshtari, N.B., Pastore, F., Goknil, A., Briand, L.C.: Metamorphic testing for web system security. IEEE Trans. Software Eng. **49**(6), 3430–3471 (2023)

3. Duque-Torres, A., Pfahl, D.: Inferring metamorphic relations from JavaDocs: a deep dive into the memo approach. In: Taibi, D., Kuhrmann, M., Mikkonen, T., Klünder, J., Abrahamsson, P. (eds.) Product-Focused Software Process Improvement, vol. 13709, pp. 418–432, Springer, Cham (2022). https://doi.org/10.1007/978-3-031-21388-5_29

4. Duque-Torres, A., Pfahl, D., Claus, K., Ramler, R.: A replication study on predicting metamorphic relations at unit testing level. In: 2022 IEEE International Conference on Software Analysis, Evolution and Reengineering (SANER), pp. 1–11 (2022)

5. Duque-Torres, A., Pfahl, D., Klammer, C., Fischer, S.: Bug or not bug? Analysing the reasons behind metamorphic relation violations. In: IEEE International Conference on Software Analysis, Evolution and Reengineering (SANER), pp. 905–912 (2023)

6. Duque-Torres, A., Pfahl, D., Klammer, C., Fischer, S.: Exploring a test data-driven method for selecting and constraining metamorphic relations. arXiv preprint arXiv:2307.15522 (2023)

7. Duque-Torres, A., Pfahl, D., Klammer, C., Fisher, S.: Using source code metrics for predicting metamorphic relations at method level. In: 5th Workshop on Validation, Analysis and Evolution of Software Tests (2022)

8. Kanewala, U., Bieman, J.M.: Using machine learning techniques to detect metamorphic relations for programs without test oracles. In: IEEE 24th International Symposium on Software Reliability Engineering (ISSRE) (2013)

9. Kanewala, U., Bieman, J.M., Ben-Hur, A.: Predicting metamorphic relations for testing scientific software: a machine learning approach using graph kernels. Softw. Test. Verification Reliab. **26**(3), 245–269 (2016)

10. Mai, P.X., Goknil, A., Pastore, F., Briand, L.C.: SMRL: a metamorphic security testing tool for web systems. In: 2020 IEEE/ACM 42nd International Conference on Software Engineering: Companion Proceedings (ICSE-Companion), pp. 9–12 (2020)

11. Mai, P.X., Pastore, F., Goknil, A., Briand, L.: Metamorphic security testing for web systems. In: 2020 IEEE 13th International Conference on Software Testing, Validation and Verification (ICST), pp. 186–197 (2020)

12. Segura, S., Fraser, G., Sanchez, A.B., Ruiz-Cortés, A.: A survey on metamorphic testing. IEEE Trans. Softw. Eng. **42**(9) (2016)

13. Xie, X., Li, J., Wang, C., Chen, T.Y.: Looking for an MR? Try METWiki today. In: 2016 IEEE/ACM 1st International Workshop on Metamorphic Testing (MET), pp. 1–4 (2016)

Author Index

R. Kadgien et al. (Eds.): PROFES 2023, LNCS 14484, pp. 153–155, 2024.
https://doi.org/10.1007/978-3-031-49269-3

Printed in the United States
by Baker & Taylor Publisher Services